Altar'd

Altar'd

THE TRANSFORMING POWER OF SURRENDER

SUSAN O. KENT

 Seedbed

Unless otherwise stated, Scripture quotations are taken from the Holy Bible, New International Version®, NIV® Copyright © 1973, 1978, 1984, 2011 by Biblica, Inc.™ Used by permission of Zondervan. All rights reserved worldwide. www.zondervan.com. The "NIV" and "New International Version" are trademarks registered in the United States Patent and Trademark Office by Biblica, Inc.™ All rights reserved worldwide.

Scripture quotations marked CEB are from the COMMON ENGLISH BIBLE. © Copyright 2011 COMMON ENGLISH BIBLE. All rights reserved. Used by permission. (www.CommonEnglishBible.com).

Scripture quotations marked AMP are taken from the Amplified® Bible (AMP), Copyright © 2015 by The Lockman Foundation. Used by permission. lockman.org.

Printed in the United States of America

Cover illustration by Nate Farro
Art direction and cover design by Nick Perreault
Page design and layout by PerfecType, Nashville, Tennessee

Kent, Susan O.
   Altar'd : the transforming power of surrender / Susan O. Kent. – Franklin, Tennessee : Seedbed Publishing, ©2023.

   pages ; cm.

   ISBN: 9798888000595 (paperback)
   ISBN: 9798888000625 (DVD)
   ISBN: 9798888000601 (epub)
   ISBN: 9798888000618 (pdf)
   OCLC: 1409624319

   1. Devotional calendars.   2. Christian life--Meditations.   3. Spiritual life—Christianity--Meditations.   4. Sacrifice--Biblical teaching.   I. Title.

BV4510.3.K46 2023   248.4   2023950807

SEEDBED PUBLISHING
Franklin, Tennessee
seedbed.com

Contents

Part Two: Surrender Control for Commitment (Burnt Offering)

Part Three: Surrender Worry for Trust (Grain Offering)

Part Four: Surrender Thanks for Peace (Peace Offering)

Part Five: Surrender Past for Freedom (Sin Offering)

Part Six: Surrender Pain for Restoration (Guilt Offering)

Foreword

One of the most vivid memories I have as a child growing up in the church was that part of the worship service when the pastor would extend an invitation for anyone to come forward if they were desiring to pray. It was known as the "altar call." And even though I didn't really know the deeper meaning and purpose of what it was all about, I could tell even at that age that it was a very special moment in the life of our congregation. Why would people line up and wait so long just to "talk to God"? In those days there wasn't a designated place for kids my age to go during church, so I went to big folks' worship with my mother and grandmother. On their way to pray, they would take me by my hand, lead me to the altar, and I would kneel beside them as they poured their hearts out to the Lord. While kneeling, I would take a quick glance to my right and to my left, and see people with eyes closed and eyes open, hands outstretched and hands folded close to their chest, seemingly surrendering themselves to a power I could neither see nor hear. Some were crying, while others were bent over and leaning on the altar like a crutch holding them up. It was magical. It was mystifying. It felt as though we were on our knees for a long time, and by the time we returned to our pew, the entire congregation was in a different place, overcome by a Spirit of surrender and release. From those experiences I came away with a profound respect for the altar, a special place where people would meet to have their conversations with God.

Now, more than six decades later, I have come across this amazing Lenten worship series and devotional study written by my good friend and colleague Rev. Susan Kent. This outstanding work has not only rekindled and revived the memories of my childhood and my respect for what an altar represents, but it has brought me into a deeper awareness that altars need not be confined to a building or a church but can literally be any special place where we can experience the presence of God and encounter our Lord and Savior Jesus Christ! What better time than the season of Lent to introduce us to embracing a life of surrender so we may draw nearer to God? This study enables us to do that through Scripture, remarkable lessons, prayers, and questions that are designed to maximize the Lenten experience.

This forty-seven-day journey is a road map for our wandering spirits and water to our thirsty souls. Reverend Kent has skillfully reimagined how we can gain a new perspective of this most sacred and holy season. Once you take the first step, you'll discover as I have that there is no turning back. This guide can be used in Sunday school classes, study groups, as a worship experience, and in many, many other ways. For me, the benchmark for any devotional study is: Does it have the capacity to change a person's life? After reading this masterful publication, I can answer that question with a resounding yes!

The altar is open—come and receive the blessing it gives!

Bishop Robert E. "Bob" Hayes Jr.
Bishop Emeritus, the Global Methodist Church

Introduction

Change.

We have a love-hate relationship with change. We want change when we start a new exercise or diet plan. We want change when we begin a new school year. We want change when we start a new job, but we don't love change when it comes at a cost. We don't love when we have to get up earlier to work out, when we can't eat our favorite foods, when we have to study rather than go out with friends, or when we have to give up the coworkers we have grown to love.

As followers of Jesus, as disciples, we want change. We want to grow deeper in our relationship with Christ. We want to be a better spouse and a better friend. We want to love more and worry less. We want to be more like Jesus, but that comes at a cost. This Lenten season, we are going to pursue change. We are going to ask the Lord to change our hearts, our minds, and our behavior so we can grow deeper, be better, and look more like Him.

In the world of fashion, changes made to clothing are called alterations. If you've ever gone to a tailor to have a hem taken up or a sleeve let out, you know that an alteration requires you to stand still so the tailor can examine the garment. You are asked to step onto a platform, stare into the mirror, and allow the expert to assess the current state of the clothing. With a trained eye, the tailor will mark the areas that need to be altered, and then with a little time and careful work, the garment will be made new and improved.

We are going to pursue a spiritual alteration this Lenten season as we seek to encounter the triune God. The truth is, God is always calling us to be changed and shaped into His image, not just during the season of Lent. In fact, He has always invited His people to encounter Him. In the Old Testament, He made a way through a tabernacle and a temple to come into His presence. He directed His people to build altars both inside and outside of the tabernacle as an intentional space to experience His presence. In the New Testament, Jesus became the living and breathing presence of God and after the resurrection, we became the temple where the Spirit of God dwells.

This Lenten season, we are asking the Lord to be the tailor. He will ask us to stand in front of the mirror to reflect on the places in our lives that need alteration. We will ask Him to assess the state of our hearts, to appraise our lives, and to mark the places that need to be reshaped. We will ask the Lord to bring a transformation and make us new again.

Now, to be clear, the Almighty Creator of the universe is not a transactional God, meaning we cannot treat Him as a vending machine where we put something in and demand something to come out. However, we can learn the rhythms of life which God Himself has provided as a way to encounter His presence. As we study God's Word, we will find that in both the Old Testament and the New Testament there are similarities when people encountered the Lord: a space was created, a sacrifice was offered, and a transformational shift was experienced. For our purposes this Lent, we will think about these three aspects: Space + Surrender = Shift

SPACE

In the Old Testament, God's people created altars. The allusion to an altar begins even before the instructions on how to build one is given. The altar was the space that was created to bring an offering as a way to honor God and encounter His presence. Altars were also built to mark a space where God spoke, gave direction, and gave His blessing. In the New Testament, Jesus became that space. It was through Jesus, the Son of God, that people were able to encounter the power and presence of the Lord in a new way. Jesus was the place for people who were hurting, lost, and who longed to experience God. Jesus also gave us an example of how to create space through prayer, silence, and solitude.

SURRENDER

In the Old Testament, God's people brought a sacrifice to the altar. They were given instructions on what to bring and how to offer it. Some of the offerings were brought to proclaim their obedience or to be consecrated for their work. Some offerings were brought as a surrender of their firstfruits, or to offer their thanksgiving. Other sacrifices were made as an atonement for their sin. In the New Testament, Jesus became the ultimate sacrifice surrendered on the cross, but Jesus also surrendered Himself daily. He surrendered His life to show others the way to restoration with the Father through humility and service.

SHIFT 3

The transformational shift we experience when we create a space to encounter God and offer our surrender to Him comes only through the power of the triune God. We may stand in the mirror and ask the Lord to change our hearts, but our true transformation comes through the work of the Holy Spirit. And if we are honest with ourselves, we long for this change because the world we live in today is not the world as God established it.

The first week we will spend time focused on the altar and the sacrifice. What does it mean to create space and to offer a surrender? Each week that follows will focus on a specific area in our lives we need to surrender like control, worry, our thanks, our past, and our pain. We will study an Old Testament offering and altar story as well as the New Testament scriptures leading us to create space and surrender our lives as followers of Jesus so we may be transformed by the Holy Spirit.

Let's begin our journey by stepping onto the platform to be *altar'd*. Allow yourself to stare into the mirror. Reflect on what you see. Do not hide your imperfections from the Tailor but give your whole self into the loving hands of the Lord who makes all things new.

Part One

The Altar and the Sacrifice

Day 1
Being Made New

2 CORINTHIANS 5:17 Therefore, if anyone is in Christ, the new creation has come: The old has gone, the new is here!

CONSIDER THIS

What does it take to make something new? First, we recognize that what it is now, is not as it once was. When we examine our lives, we must consider God's original intention for His creation. Let's go back to the beginning. When God created the universe and formed the heavens and the earth, there was no separation of the two. "On earth as it is in heaven" was a reality. His Spirit hovered. He created day and night, land and water, plants and animals, and His creation was good. Then He created man and woman and it was very good. God created heaven on earth and His creation was in perfect relationship with Him. It was just as He envisioned.

But as God's creation succumbed to the temptation of sin, the earth no longer looked like heaven. The weaving of lies and the twisting of truth spoiled the creation of God. The earth we experience is not the perfect communion God originally created, but it is also not the end of the story. The earth longs for its Creator and stretches out to find the relationship it once had. Our deepest longing is, and should be, to once again experience heaven on earth.

In what some call Paul's most personal letter, the truth we find in 2 Corinthians should be the foundation and motivation for our Lenten journey. He writes that if *anyone* is in Christ, they are made new, which means there is nothing in your past or present that will keep you from experiencing the transforming power of the Lord. We begin today, on Ash Wednesday, to place ourselves before Jesus, asking Him to examine our hearts and allowing us to confess the sins in our lives. We do this because being made new means being honest with what needs to be changed.

In the midst of a world filled with chaos and disappointment, pain and death, there is a promise of restoration and transformation through Jesus. And the good news is transformation isn't found at the end of our lives, but at the end of ourselves. This is the beauty of the Lenten season. It's a season in the church calendar where most of us, perhaps more intentionally than any other time, commit to seek transformation. We search the Scriptures and sit in stillness with God as we recognize the sin which has broken the perfect communion

God created. We long to be transformed into the image of our Savior who has given His life so we can once again experience earth as it is in heaven, God's kingdom. That is the promise of Jesus. It is the fulfillment of God's design.

Let us seek transformation, not for the purpose of finding happiness or avoiding pain, putting on an appearance of success, or storing up treasures for our own gain. Let us seek transformation to experience an awakening of holiness within ourselves and encounter the power of our risen Savior to radically alter the way we live.

THE PRAYER

Lord, search us and draw our attention to those places in our lives which need Your forgiveness and transforming power. Don't let us stay the way we are, but renew us, fill us, and change us so we can reflect Your grace in this world. Amen

THE QUESTIONS

- What fear or concerns do you have as you give yourself over to the Lord to be changed?
- What is your hope for transformation as you embrace the promise of being made new?
- What do you need to confess to the Lord today?

Day 2
Let's Make an Altar

GENESIS 8:15-20 Then God said to Noah, "Come out of the ark, you and your wife and your sons and their wives. Bring out every kind of living creature that is with you—the birds, the animals, and all the creatures that move along the ground—so they can multiply on the earth and be fruitful and increase in number on it."

So Noah came out, together with his sons and his wife and his sons' wives. All the animals and all the creatures that move along the ground and all the birds—everything that moves on land—came out of the ark, one kind after another.

Then Noah built an altar to the Lord and, taking some of all the clean animals and clean birds, he sacrificed burnt offerings on it.

CONSIDER THIS

Chances are you remember receiving news reports and mandates to shelter in place as the COVID-19 virus was spreading rapidly through our world. After days, weeks, and months, the hardships of what we had to sacrifice as a result of the pandemic became more of a reality. Not only did we give up in-person church gatherings, but family celebrations and even mundane tasks like grocery shopping. For some, complete isolation was required. Then, slowly, doors were opened and we were given permission to go out and experience creation and community once again. Many of us desired to share meals with others and to see each other in 3-D rather than on a screen. It was what our heart longed for so we made it a priority.

When Noah received word that his family could leave the ark and experience the world again, what did he do? He built an altar. His heart longed to create a space where he could encounter the presence of God. Remember that the ark was given to Noah and his family as a saving grace to escape the punishment of sin. The flood came because humans had completely given in to their desires and God wanted to wipe away everything that had degraded His creation. The flood washed away the sin, but it also showed the power of God to provide salvation.

Place yourself on that ark. Can you imagine the conversations Noah had with his family? What did they long for most? Did they remember the times they were distracted by the world and tempted to follow what others were doing? As they saw the world washed away, were they were filled with sadness for what was lost and gratitude for God's protection? Did they look around and give thanks for all the God had provided for them even in the confinement of the ark? Forty days and forty nights of rain and reflection created a longing for God, a longing to encounter the one who had saved them, a longing to give back to God what He had provided to them. So, Noah built an altar.

As we begin this Lenten season, what will our heart long for during these days and nights? It's our time to build an altar with our lives. Let's use these days to create a space where our longing hearts can dwell with God. Let's reflect on our own sin and surrender ourselves to His mercy. Let's pray for and experience the transformation that comes as we shift our minds and our hearts through the power of the Holy Spirit. Let's explore more deeply each of these so we can be altar'd through the grace of God.

THE PRAYER

Mighty God, You are our Provider, our Savior, our Redeemer. We long for You. Our days and weeks drift by and we miss Your presence. We give ourselves to You and pray for the transforming power of the Holy Spirit. Amen.

THE QUESTIONS

- What does your heart long for right now?
- How can you begin to create an altar in your life, a space to encounter the triune God?

Day 3
Fan the Flame

LEVITICUS 6:8-9 The Lᴏʀᴅ said to Moses: "Give Aaron and his sons this command: 'These are the regulations for the burnt offering: The burnt offering is to remain on the altar hearth throughout the night, till morning, and the fire must be kept burning on the altar.'"

CONSIDER THIS

Yesterday we began building an altar with our lives, and today we will learn that the altar fire must be kept burning. What does that mean? First, let's admit that many of us have not put the book of Leviticus on the top of our reading lists. It might be that it doesn't seem relevant. If you skim through the pages, the topics of skin diseases, priests, and festivals do not seem to be important to us thousands of years after it was written. I understand. Leviticus provided rules and guidelines for the Israelites after they had been rescued from slavery in Egypt and it taught them how to live practically as a reflection of their faith in the one true God. Within these guidelines are lessons about altars and offerings. They remind us of the temporary system God gave His people, but they also teach us how Jesus's life and resurrection became our ultimate offering and the fulfillment of God's covenant.

What does the Lord tell Moses about the fire for the altar? It must be kept burning. Growing up, as I watched TV, there was a commercial for a hotel chain that ended with, "We'll keep the light on for you." It conveyed a constant vigilance and readiness to welcome the guest whenever they arrived. If our lives are to be an altar, we need to stay vigilant and be ready for when the Lord returns. Each Old Testament altar would require a fire to consume the offering, and it would be up to the priest to tend to the flame. It would have been fairly easy to keep the fire burning when the offering was first placed on the altar, but to maintain the fire throughout the day and night would have meant a constant watch. The priest couldn't set the offering on the altar and walk away or get distracted. He couldn't check on the fire one day a week or when it was convenient. He had to fan the flame to remain alert and ready to encounter the presence of God.

Being a follower of Jesus means we are also asked to fan the flame of our spiritual lives. The disciples didn't clock in from 9 to 5 and take the weekends off. We cannot pop into church and check the box of weekly worship or monthly giving. We must fan the flame and attend to the fire on a daily basis so we may experience the fullness of life in Christ. The apostle Paul, a follower of Jesus who wrote and influenced many of the books in the New Testament, warned other believers to "not quench the spirit" (1 Thess. 5:19). Think of a campfire which has dirt or ash strewn on it. The flame will be diminished and could go out. When we are inconsistent in spending time with Jesus, it's like dampening a fire with ash so the heat does not reach as far as it once did and the fuel doesn't burn as brightly.

How brightly are you burning right now? Where has ash been thrown on the fire of your spiritual life? When we fan the flame with our attentiveness, we become ready to respond as the Holy Spirit leads us and we become light to those around us.

THE PRAYER

Lord, there are days when it feels like the fire of Your presence is just a little smoke coming from smoldering ash. Forgive us when we have taken Your presence for granted and we have not been attentive in our prayer lives. Amen.

THE QUESTIONS

- In what ways are you quenching the Spirit by not attending to your spiritual life?
- What will you do this week to fan the flame of your altar?

Day 4
Space, the Final Frontier

EPHESIANS 3:14-19 For this reason I kneel before the Father, from whom every family in heaven and on earth derives its name. I pray that out of his glorious riches he may strengthen you with power through his Spirit in your inner being, so that Christ may dwell in your hearts through faith. And I pray that you, being rooted and established in love, may have power, together with all the Lord's holy people, to grasp how wide and long and high and deep is the love of Christ, and to know this love that surpasses knowledge—that you may be filled to the measure of all the fullness of God.

CONSIDER THIS

If you ever get a chance to watch one of the 20,000 (okay, probably an exaggeration) home improvement shows, pay attention to the computer-generated interior design programs. They are fascinating. The designer can literally imagine hundreds of different ways to utilize the space he is given. He can rearrange furniture, remove cabinets, and raise the ceiling. Sometimes he will even take down walls to create a larger space. The goal for the designer is to create a physical space that reflects the heart of the family who lives there. This is the same goal for an altar. It's a physical space that reflects the longing of a heart to encounter God. Let's look at the physical space we have created and how it reflects our own hearts.

In today's passage, the apostle Paul is praising God for all that He has done to unify the believers under Jesus. He gives thanks to God for bringing all people together into the family of God through the Spirit. When Jesus fulfilled God's covenant through His death and resurrection, the walls of restrictive laws of the Torah were taken down and there was room made in the family of God for Gentiles (non-Jews). Like a beautiful renovation, space was made for all people. Paul then prayed for the believers to make space in their lives so that Jesus could dwell in their hearts and they could be transformed by the Holy Spirit.

I love that Paul used the word *dwell*, which in Greek is *katoikeō* and means "to inhabit" or "settle." This imagery paints a picture for us that is helpful to understand Paul's prayer. There is a difference between occupying a space and dwelling in a space. If you have ever moved into an apartment or a dorm, you most likely moved in with a mindset that it wouldn't be permanent. You may have been hesitant to hang photos on the wall or bring all of your belongings. You moved in, but you didn't settle in.

However, if you have ever purchased a home, you probably moved in with a different mindset. You wanted to dwell in that space, to settle in. You wanted to paint the walls and hang pictures. You wanted to make it your own because it was permanent. Paul's prayer for the Ephesians is that they would allow Jesus to permanently settle into their hearts and dwell there so they could be filled to the measure of all the fullness of God.

Is Jesus fully settled in your heart? As an altar, our lives become the space where the Holy Spirit dwells and those around us see evidence of God's presence. Have you created space for the Lord in your heart and also in the physical space of your home, work, or school? During this Lenten journey, we may need to do a little remodeling so Jesus can dwell more fully in the altar of our lives.

THE PRAYER

Jesus, as we kneel before You, we pray for the Holy Spirit to come and dwell in us. Fill us to overflowing with Your grace and mercy so we may be a witness to others. Amen.

THE QUESTIONS

- Does it feel like Jesus dwells in your heart? If you are unsure, consider what space you have made for Him.
- What are some physical reminders around you that reflect your devotion to Jesus?

Day 5
Head Space

COLOSSIANS 3:1-3 Since, then, you have been raised with Christ, set your hearts on things above, where Christ is, seated at the right hand of God. Set your minds on things above, not on earthly things. For you died, and your life is now hidden with Christ in God.

CONSIDER THIS

Have you ever walked around your house looking for the perfect Wi-Fi spot for your cell phone? You know, the place where reception is crystal clear and there is nothing interfering? There are times when I've wandered around my home and dropped important phone conversations because my reception was bad. If I'm being honest, that could also describe my spiritual life. However, when that happens, I find that it is not God who has lost transmission, but my wandering mind which has lost reception.

As we build our lives as an altar, we need to create mental space and set our minds on Christ. We can have the most beautiful chapels for worship and our homes can have the most serene devotional space, but if our minds are not set, we can be like the Israelites wandering in the desert. In our passage, Paul wrote to the Colossians to encourage them. They were distracted by noise of the world, and he told them to set their hearts and their minds on things above. The definition of the word *set* in the original language gives us a little more insight. To set means to direct one's mind or to seek. In other words, this is not a passive activity.

I know that when I am not actively engaging my mind or directing it toward a particular activity then it is guaranteed to wander, and it typically wanders to a streaming service or a game on my phone. Paul knew that the world is always offering distractions for a wandering mind so the only way to live as a faithful disciple is to actively direct our minds toward Jesus. When our hearts and minds are on Christ, our lives will reflect Christ. Theologian A. W. Tozer wrote, "the [person] who would know God must give time to Him."[1]

Setting our minds on the things above can be easier said than done. As we seek to be altar'd during this Lenten season, we may need to make two changes: reset and replace. First, let's reset. Creating mental space might mean physically moving to a space that is more conducive for your mind to

---

1. A. W. Tozer, *The Divine Conquest* (Carol Stream, IL: Tyndale, 1995).

focus. Jesus would often leave the crowds and the activity of the town to pray alone. "Very early in the morning, while it was still dark, Jesus got up, left the house and went off to a solitary place, where he prayed" (Mark 1:35). He had to reset by physically leaving a place to mentally create space.

Second, let's replace. Creating mental space might mean replacing what is normal in our routine for a different activity. We may need to replace something that is trivial with something that is meaningful. Replace something that is draining with something that is filling. What is taking up your mental space today? The world is not lacking for things that can distract us and drain us, but we have a choice to reset and replace so that our time can be offered to the Lord.

THE PRAYER

Lord, be the only clear voice in our heads today. We choose to set our minds on the good news of Christ so we can set our hearts and minds on You. Amen.

THE QUESTIONS

- What is the noise in your life that distracts you?
- How does the physical space you create help provide time for mental space? Are there any changes you can make in your life today that give more time for God?

Day 6
The Sacrifice

1 PETER 2:23-24 When they hurled their insults at him, he did not retaliate; when he suffered, he made no threats. Instead, he entrusted himself to him who judges justly. "He himself bore our sins" in his body on the cross, so that we might die to sins and live for righteousness; "by his wounds you have been healed."

CONSIDER THIS

When choosing a hero, my mind dreams up images of warriors. Men and women who have protective clothing and perhaps a shield or specialized weapons at their ready. My heroes stand in a position of offense, knees bent, body leaning forward, where at any moment they will spring into action to defend themselves against the enemy. But this is not the image Jesus offers us. The image we are given of Jesus is that of a sacrifice.

He took the insults, ridicule, and hatred of others. In case you think their insults bounced off Him like Ironman, be sure to read carefully. He suffered. Being fully human and fully divine, Jesus felt the pain inflicted by others. He heard the hatred and He felt the abuse. And when He suffered, He did not return evil for evil. He entrusted Himself to God.

The English version of this passage loses a little in translation. The word for *entrusted* is written in an imperfect tense, which means we should read "he *continually* entrusted himself *each time*" to God. Jesus did not experience being hurt just once. He didn't stand His ground just one time and He didn't declare victory after one attack. He repeatedly surrendered Himself. When an animal was offered as a sacrifice, it was physically surrendered. Jesus became the sacrifice and surrendered His life for us.

Our lives are not only an altar, but we are to share in the sufferings of Christ which means we also offer ourselves as a sacrifice. There will be times when we feel the pain of insults and we are wounded by others, but our response is to mirror the response of Jesus. We must spiritually, emotionally, and physically surrender ourselves, entrusting our lives to God.

The Greek word for surrender is *paradidomi* and it means to commit, yield, and entrust. In many ways I see the kingdom version of surrender as an exchange. When we entrust our lives to God, He gives something back. When we commit our ways, He fills us. When we yield our wills, He directs us. When we entrust ourselves to the Lord, He gives us life. It is only in the upside-down nature of God's kingdom that surrender is encouraged. In our world, most of us would rather have the body armor and the weapons because our culture says surrendering means losing, being defeated, being the weaker person. It's being put into the loser bracket. And yet, it was from a posture of surrender that Jesus won eternal life for you and me. By His wounds we are healed.

There's a reason our superheroes have protective clothing and specialized weapons. Without them they are merely human. They can be hurt and even die. On our own, when people hurl insults and hurt us, our natural desire is to return the favor by throwing it back. However, our supernatural defense comes through the Spirit of Christ who showed us how to embrace a life of surrender and entrust our response to God. We offer our own sacrifice and we receive the Lord's salvation.

THE PRAYER

Lord, You have shown us that the strongest position we can take is the position of surrender. We entrust all that we have and all that we are to You. Amen.

THE QUESTIONS

- What comfort do you receive when you read, "By his wounds you have been healed"?
- In what ways can you view surrender as a position of strength?

Day 7
CTRL + ALT + DEL

MATTHEW 7:24-27 "Therefore everyone who hears these words of mine and puts them into practice is like a wise man who built his house on the rock. The rain came down, the streams rose, and the winds blew and beat against that house; yet it did not fall, because it had its foundation on the rock. But everyone who hears these words of mine and does not put them into practice is like a foolish man who built his house on sand. The rain came down, the streams rose, and the winds blew and beat against that house, and it fell with a great crash."

CONSIDER THIS

For those of us who grew up using an archaic piece of machinery called a typewriter, we can fully appreciate the brilliant advancements in technology we have called *short-cuts*. These shortcuts are the keys for a computer that allow you to delete or copy or undo what you just did with a simple key stroke. When I learned how to use a typewriter (yes there were actual classes for that) we had to practice over and over again to increase our efficiency and reduce our mistakes. When a mistake was made or we wanted to undo what we just did, we had to rip the sheet out of the typewriter and start from the beginning. If you were lucky, some of the newer typewriters had a correction tape that would allow you to white out a few letters or a word, but it did not always work well. In our spiritual lives, as we grow in maturity as disciples, the truth is, there are no shortcuts, just practice.

As Jesus was preaching His Sermon on the Mount, He gave an illustration of the wise man versus the foolish man. In that sermon, Jesus was giving practical direction on how to live a faithful life as a disciple. He begins by offering blessings and then gives instructions on how to respond to God's gift of grace. There's no Oprah moment of "you get a car, and you get a car, and you . . ." without an expected response. Did you catch the important phrase? "And puts them into practice." Jesus had finished teaching on how to be blessed, how to treat others, how to pray, and how to seek God, but hearing His words would mean nothing if they did not put them into practice.

You can want to be a great pitcher, but if you don't practice, you will never grow as a baseball player. You can be inspired by a great sermon, but if you don't put the lessons into practice, you're not living as a disciple. You can want to hear the voice of the Lord in your prayer, but if you do not pray daily, you'll not experience the gift of His presence. The wise man took Jesus's teachings and he built his house (life) on the rocks so when the troubles of the world came, he was prepared. It won't be easy to build our house. We'll make mistakes. We'll abandon our daily walks with Christ. But the house can still be built. It will take a lifetime to follow Jesus's teaching, but if we want to be altar'd, there are no shortcut keys to discipleship. Surrendering takes practice.

THE PRAYER

Lord, we know You have made a way for us to build a strong house. On the days when we want a shortcut, let us remember that You did not take the easy way out to give us salvation. We don't ever want to take for granted the life You have offered us. Amen.

THE QUESTIONS

- How are you already putting into practice something you have learned from this Lenten devotional?
- What are some of the ways you have faced the "wind and the rain" of life? How has being a follower of Jesus helped you face those trials?

Day 8

Promises, Promises

EXODUS 24:3-7 When Moses went and told the people all the Lord's words and laws, they responded with one voice, "Everything the Lord has said we will do." Moses then wrote down everything the Lord had said.

He got up early the next morning and built an altar at the foot of the mountain and set up twelve stone pillars representing the twelve tribes of Israel. Then he sent young Israelite men, and they offered burnt offerings and sacrificed young bulls as fellowship offerings to the Lord. Moses took half of the blood and put it in bowls, and the other half he splashed against the altar. Then he took the Book of the Covenant and read it to the people. They responded, "We will do everything the Lord has said; we will obey."

CONSIDER THIS

Have you ever made a promise you didn't keep? Growing up, our family followed the tradition of giving something up during Lent and we carried that through with our own kids. Several of us typically chose a favorite food (mine was usually dessert) or a favorite activity and I always started out the Lenten season strong. The first week after Ash Wednesday I could stare down a piece of pie or an ice cream sundae with great resolve. The second and third weeks of Lent got a little tough because my husband's birthday almost always fell during Lent and I began to have conversations with myself. "Well, I'm sure God wouldn't mind if we cheated on the 'no dessert' promise just a little so we could celebrate, right? And we really need to celebrate with his parents too so maybe just a couple of times is okay. And the Sundays are supposed to be 'little Easters' so maybe I can just borrow those days and use them during the week." Have you ever struggled with Lenten promises like I have?

In our passage today, we join the Israelites in the desert. They have been freed from slavery to the Egyptians and God has given them His presence through a cloud by day and a pillar of fire by night. They have received miraculous provision from God in the form of manna, quail, and water. They have been given God's direction through His commandments on how to live faithfully. What was their response? Moses built an altar to offer a sacrifice and the people made a promise. "Everything the Lord has said, we will do!"

They surrendered themselves by offering a promise to God. They offered their obedience, not once, but twice. I want to believe that as they gathered and heard Moses read the words of the God, they were truly sincere in their promise just like I was with surrendering dessert during Lent. I want to believe that they meant the words they spoke aloud. Yet, if you have read much of the Old Testament, you already know that the promise of obedience did not last long.

How are you in making promises to God? Sometimes I find it easy to make a promise in the moment like when God pours out His blessings. *Yes, Lord! I will obey You. Yes, Lord, I will go where You lead me and love my enemy and give sacrificially.* But I'm not sure I'm much better than the Israelites in keeping my promises.

In the Gospel of Matthew, Jesus says "or the mouth speaks what the heart is full of" (Matt. 12:34). Our words are important because they reflect what is in our heart. Do our promises reflect our commitment to the Lord or do we treat our words as if they hold no weight? Do we toss around promises like cotton candy that disappear the instant they are consumed?

We may have begun this Lenten season with a promise to spend daily time in prayer or to sacrifice a favorite food, but perhaps we should start with surrendering our promise and ask God to help us keep it.

THE PRAYER

Lord, may the words of our mouths reflect the love and devotion we have in our hearts for You. As flawed people, we know that we cannot keep all the promises we speak, but with the help of the Holy Spirit, we can. Amen.

THE QUESTIONS

- In what ways have you seen the words of your mouth reflecting what is in your heart?
- What is a promise you can make for this Lenten season that reflects your love for God?

Day 9
Captain Obvious

GALATIANS 5:19-21 The acts of the flesh are obvious: sexual immorality, impurity and debauchery; idolatry and witchcraft; hatred, discord, jealousy, fits of rage, selfish ambition, dissensions, factions and envy; drunkenness, orgies, and the like. I warn you, as I did before, that those who live like this will not inherit the kingdom of God.

CONSIDER THIS

Whether you've heard it said or seen a reference to the phrase "captain obvious," the meaning is, well, obvious. We use the phrase to refer to certain situations which do not require elaboration. Yesterday, we spent time considering how we can surrender our promises. Today, Paul addresses an opportunity to surrender some obviously bad habits.

In his letter to the Galatians, Paul affirms that because of grace through Jesus, believers have been given a life of freedom. That's the good news of Jesus. Those who have confessed faith in Christ are not bound to the penalty of sin because Jesus has paid the price. However, Paul warns them that their freedom does not mean they are free to behave any way they choose. They must deny acts of the flesh because the way believers live is a reflection of Christ. Just as what comes out of the mouth reflects our hearts, our actions reflect our lives as followers of Jesus.

As we skim Paul's list, we may be tempted to brush it aside and claim that those are sins we would obviously not commit. Surely, we can all agree not to participate in debauchery, idolatry, and witchcraft. However, if we look at Paul's list in the New Living Translation, which uses more common language, we see that we are not free to lose our temper, to be selfish, or to be jealous. Being a southerner, I'd say that Paul is just meddlin'!

Believers who are practicing the way of Christ must surrender any habits that do not reflect their lives of freedom. We must make choices. Author Stephen R. Covey, the well-known author of *The 7 Habits of Highly Effective People* puts it this way, "[we] are not the product of [our] circumstances. [We] are the product of [our] decisions."[2] If we are going to be altar'd this Lenten season, we need to be intentional in surrendering our habits. We need to be willing to place in front of God, those acts of the flesh which do not reflect the

---

2. Stephen R. Covey, *The 7 Habits of Highly Effective People: Restoring the Character Ethic* (New York: Simon & Schuster, 2014).

nature of Christ. Jesus did not give Himself up for us so we can abuse the freedom and continue to act as though we have not been released from sin.

THE PRAYER

Lord, may the way we live outwardly reflect the love and commitment we have made to You. We surrender to You our full selves so that what people see is a witness to Your character. Amen.

THE QUESTIONS

- Why do you think Paul felt it necessary to list examples of acts of the flesh to the Galatians and why might that lesson be for us?
- What is an obvious example in your own life of an action which does not reflect Christ? Are you willing to surrender it today?

Day 10

Are We There Yet?

JOHN 13:15 "I have set you an example that you should do as I have done for you."

CONSIDER THIS

It can be tempting to always look at the big picture, the five-year vision, or the end goal whether you are in corporate America, running a household, or just planning your life. It's exciting to think about how great life will be when you see the vision fulfilled and you meet the goal. Don't get me wrong, visioning is critical because you need to know what you want and where you are going, but there is no five-year vision without a daily plan to get there. You cannot cross the finish line without taking every step beginning at the starting gate, and we cannot be transformed if we do not surrender on a daily basis.

Today's passage is short. You may be celebrating that fact or you may have thought we made a mistake accidentally deleting some verses. But today, I want us to marinate on these few words because they are deeply important. Every change in behavior, attitude, and heart begins with a desire, and it is only accomplished by making a choice every day to get there.

These words were spoken by Jesus to His disciples the last week of His life. Jesus had proven His authority and He had predicted His death and resurrection. Now, as He spent a meal with them, He demonstrated an act of service and then said these words, "I have set you an example that you should do as I have done for you." He had given the example to follow. Not just what they observed that night, but every day they walked with Him and healed and taught and ministered to others. He was the example. They did not have to wonder what to do; they just had to follow.

As a young student learns to write, they are not given a blank sheet of paper and told to write the alphabet. No, they are given an example. They have lined paper as boundaries and they have dotted lines to follow in the shape of the letter they want to form. Each day they follow the example. Each day their lines become straighter and cleaner and are made with more confidence. As the days pass, they will be able to draw the letters without the dots. And then the paper will have less lines. Daily they practice and daily they become more like the example until one day they can write the alphabet on a blank sheet of paper.

Pastor Eugene Peterson, quoting Friedrich Nietzsche, might describe this daily practice of being altar'd as a "long obedience in the same direction."[3] It is only when we choose a life of daily surrender that we will fulfill the vision and accomplish the goal set before us. If you read the Gospels, you will find that Jesus gave us many examples of how to live:

"Follow me."

"This is how you pray."

"Go and make disciples."

May we embrace a life of daily surrender that Jesus left as an example.

THE PRAYER

Lord, forgive us for not following Your example. Forgive us for each time we have not served and loved like You did. Continue to teach us how to live every day as a reflection of You. Amen.

THE QUESTIONS

- What is one example that Jesus gave us that you want to practice this week?
- Where have you failed to follow the example of Jesus?

---

3. Eugene H. Peterson, *A Long Obedience in the Same Direction: Discipleship in an Instant Society* (Downers Grove, IL: InterVarsity Press, 2019).

Day 11
Forever Changed

EPHESIANS 2:1-5 As for you, you were dead in your transgressions and sins, in which you used to live when you followed the ways of this world and of the ruler of the kingdom of the air, the spirit who is now at work in those who are disobedient. All of us also lived among them at one time, gratifying the cravings of our flesh and following its desires and thoughts. Like the rest, we were by nature deserving of wrath. But because of his great love for us, God, who is rich in mercy, made us alive with Christ even when we were dead in transgressions—it is by grace you have been saved.

CONSIDER THIS

In the healing story of the blind man, Jesus asked, "What do you want me to do for you?" (Mark 10:51). We're eleven days into this Lenten journey and when we began, I said we wanted to be changed, we wanted to be altar'd by embracing a life of surrender. Is this what you want Jesus to do for you? Today's passage tells us the good news that we are not just changed, but we are *forever* changed!

Read the passage again but this time change the pronouns to make it personal. "As for me, I was dead in my transgressions and sin, in which I used to live when I followed the ways of this world and of the ruler of the kingdom of the air, the spirit who is now at work in those who are disobedient . . ." Keep going! It's good news! The transformation that God is capable of doing in your life and mine is radical and it is eternal. When we make our lives an altar and choose each day to surrender, we will forever be changed.

Paul is quite direct with his words in this letter. He tells the believers that they, like him, were deserving of wrath. That's the nature of humanity. We were sinners and we are sinners. *But God.* That can stand as a powerful sentence on its own. But God did not leave us as sinners to receive the punishment we deserved. But God did not turn His back on us. But God who is rich in mercy, perhaps better translated abounding in mercy, saved us. And this is a mercy that meets us again and again as we surrender through confession and obedience to God. When we fail, and we will, we can remember that God is rich in His mercy and His mercies are "new every morning" (Lam. 3:23).

What does Paul say God does because of His mercy? He makes us alive with Christ. The beauty of being alive, just like God's mercy, is that we can experience this daily. In another of Paul's letters he calls it walking "in newness of life" (Rom. 6:4 CEB). And all of this comes as the gift of grace we have received because Jesus surrendered His life on a cross for us. It is the only reason we can be forever changed.

Breathe in this good word today and give thanks for the mercy of God. Since Ash Wednesday we have looked at altars, altar fires, the sacrifice, and surrendering. As we continue in this journey, we will dive a little deeper into specific areas of our lives we need to surrender and what God gives us in exchange. But for today, rest in the "but God" that has changed us from being dead in our transgressions to alive with Christ.

THE PRAYER

God, we do not deserve Your mercy, but thank You for saving us. Your mercy lifts us up from the pit that we deserve to breathing in the air of the Holy Spirit. We celebrate that today. Amen.

THE QUESTIONS

- Knowing that you were dead because of your sin, how does that affect the way you approach God?
- How will you walk in newness of life this week as a sign of being alive with Christ?

Part Two

Surrender Control for Commitment (Burnt Offering)

Day 12

The Chicken or the Pig

LEVITICUS 1:1-3 The LORD called to Moses and spoke to him from the tent of meeting. He said, "Speak to the Israelites and say to them: 'When anyone among you brings an offering to the LORD, bring as your offering an animal from either the herd or the flock.

"'If the offering is a burnt offering from the herd, you are to offer a male without defect. You must present it at the entrance to the tent of meeting so that it will be acceptable to the LORD.'"

CONSIDER THIS

Have you ever had a young child come to your door asking for food donations because they were doing a service project for the local food pantry? Confession time. I have been known, in the past, to go into the kitchen and collect the cans of beans and peas that no one in the family wanted and hand them over to the young person at my door as if I was making an important contribution to the cause. How embarrassing to admit that I chose the least desired items as my offering to a local organization whose sole purpose was to feed hungry families.

This is a new week in our Lenten journey and we will focus on being altar'd by surrendering control and embracing complete commitment. In the book of Leviticus, we read about five different offerings which God asked the Israelites to place on their altar as a sacrifice. The first and most often provided was the burnt offering, or the *'olah*. In the passage, the Lord specifically required a male without defect which would have required them to let go of something of great value. Depending on the circumstances, it might have even been painful to surrender this animal to God and if we are honest, it is often feels painful to let go of control of our lives. Yet God asked His people to willingly surrender their best, not the can of lima beans from the back of the pantry.

The burnt offering would have been not only the best but would have been complete. It required that every part of the offering was given as a sacrifice, and nothing was held back. It's the difference between a chicken and a pig. Perhaps you've heard the story of the chicken and the pig who wanted to go into business together. They decided to open a breakfast shop where they would offer eggs and bacon. It didn't take long before they realized that for their business to be successful, the chicken would be involved through her activity, but the pig would be committed through his sacrifice.

For our lives to be transformed, we must embrace a life of surrender through our complete commitment. Jesus, as He was being questioned by the teachers of the law on which is the greatest commandment, quoted God's words to Moses saying, "Love the Lord your God with all your heart and with all your soul and with all your strength" (Deut. 6:5). Did you notice the word "all"? As Christ-followers, we are asked to be like a burnt offering, laying our whole selves on the altar and not holding anything back. We are to give our best and to give our all. This journey of the Lenten season prepares us for our everyday walk with Christ. To be changed and consumed by the Lord, we must be willing to surrender control and embrace commitment.

THE PRAYER

Lord, we want to be wholly consumed by You. Help us learn how to surrender ourselves to You completely so we may be used by You for Your glory. Amen.

THE QUESTIONS

- What would your best offering look like today? Are you willing to hand it over to God without any reservations?
- Why do you think God would ask for something of such high worth and not leave it up to us to decide what to give?

Day 13
The Whole Kit and Caboodle

GENESIS 22:1-2, 6-14 Some time later God tested Abraham. He said to him, "Abraham!"

"Here I am," he replied.

Then God said, "Take your son, your only son, whom you love—Isaac—and go to the region of Moriah. Sacrifice him there as a burnt offering on a mountain I will show you."...

Abraham took the wood for the burnt offering and placed it on his son Isaac, and he himself carried the fire and the knife. As the two of them went on together, Isaac spoke up and said to his father Abraham, "Father?"

"Yes, my son?" Abraham replied.

"The fire and wood are here," Isaac said, "but where is the lamb for the burnt offering?"

Abraham answered, "God himself will provide the lamb for the burnt offering, my son." And the two of them went on together.

When they reached the place God had told him about, Abraham built an altar there and arranged the wood on it. He bound his son Isaac and laid him on the altar, on top of the wood. Then he reached out his hand and took the knife to slay his son. But the angel of the L ORD called out to him from heaven, "Abraham! Abraham!"

"Here I am," he replied.

"Do not lay a hand on the boy," he said. "Do not do anything to him. Now I know that you fear God, because you have not withheld from me your son, your only son."

Abraham looked up and there in a thicket he saw a ram caught by its horns. He went over and took the ram and sacrificed it as a burnt offering instead of his son. So Abraham called that place The L ORD Will Provide. And to this day it is said, "On the mountain of the L ORD it will be provided."

CONSIDER THIS

Abraham's altar story is an incredible one. Here, at this space which was created to encounter God, Abraham was asked to surrender the very child the Lord had provided after decades of unanswered prayers. This may be the fear many of us have. If I commit my life to Him, what will God ask of me? If I promise to surrender, will He take everything I love away from me?

Putting ourselves in the story, I imagine that Abraham's feet felt like lead weights as he walked toward the place where he would build an altar. I wonder, while on his way, did his eyes scour the path, looking for signs that God would intervene?

Surely, God would not take my son away. If this altar scene were in a Hollywood production, the music score would build and the actor playing Abraham would slowly raise the knife with a dramatic pause as his arms reached their full height. There would be a tight cut away on Abraham's face and then Isaac's as the audience sat on the edge of their seats waiting to see how the climactic moment would end. And God does intervene. But not until Abraham shows that he is willing to surrender everything to the unknown future. You see, Isaac represented the future promises of his descendants. He represented the promise that God made to always be with him and to protect and provide a family. If Abraham surrendered Isaac, he was surrendering the assurance of his future.

At several pivotal moments in my faith journey, the Lord has stretched me, allowed me to suffer and asked me to surrender my future. Each time He spoke the same words to me, "You have to let go of what you have to receive what I have for you." The Lord knows that I have a hard time letting go with *both* hands. Sure, I can let go with one, but both is hard. Surrendering everything. It means completely letting go of the perceived control I have over my life. But control is an illusion. We believe if we hold on to control, we hold on to our future. But God calls us to lay our future into His hands through our faith.

God's faithfulness and love for His children creates a safe space to be vulnerable. This is a surrendered heart posture, to be open and vulnerable before the Lord who will not take everything away from us but provide our greatest need. I love that Abraham marked this sacred space where he encountered God. It was a pivotal moment in his faith journey where he surrendered his greatest possession and greatest fear to the Lord. He let go with both hands.

THE PRAYER

Lord, help us to let go with both hands. We give up the idea that we are in control because we know that You have the best for us and we commit ourselves to You. Amen.

THE QUESTIONS

- What moments of your life have you been afraid to surrender your future to God?
- What does the provision of God to Abraham teach you about God's faithfulness in your own life?

Day 14

Carry Your Cross

MATTHEW 16:22-24 Peter took him aside and began to rebuke him. "Never, Lord!" he said. "This shall never happen to you!"

Jesus turned and said to Peter, "Get behind me, Satan! You are a stumbling block to me; you do not have in mind the concerns of God, but merely human concerns."

Then Jesus said to his disciples, "Whoever wants to be my disciple must deny themselves and take up their cross and follow me."

CONSIDER THIS

Have you ever wanted to be in two places at once? Maybe you received two invitations for the same day and the same time. You wished you could say yes to both, but you knew it was impossible. You had to make a choice.

As Jesus begins to invite the disciples into the knowledge of what would happen to Him, Peter reacts forcefully, standing his ground. But Jesus responds with just as much force telling the disciples that they have to make a choice. They cannot want what is divine and what is human. They must deny one of these thoughts. The gospel writer uses the word *thelō*, which is more than just a mental decision made by weighing two options. It's a heart decision. Jesus is asking about the desire of our hearts. Surrendering control requires us to release our desire. *Does your heart long to come after Me?*

The disciples had to make a choice. They could not follow Jesus and follow themselves at the same time. That would be like having two different maps to two different locations and trying to follow both at the same time. If any wish to come after Him, they must let go of the wish to control their own plans and be willing to follow Jesus wherever that may lead. How many of us try to pursue earthly gains and spiritual gains simultaneously? The truth is, we cannot hold two desires at the same time. This doesn't mean that we won't enjoy success in our lives and businesses, but only one pursuit can control our minds and our hearts.

But this surrender doesn't just ask us to lay down our lives and our desires. No, we also have something to pick up. It asks us to willingly pick up our cross. Just as the cross became the instrument of Jesus's earthly death, it becomes the place of our own death. Death to controlling our lives. Death to our own plans. The cross is an intentional and daily commitment to give up control of our lives for the sake of Christ.

Jesus asked His disciples to make a choice. Every person will come to a point when they, too, must make the same choice, which is probably why my favorite verse in Scripture is in Paul's letter to the Philippians, "For to me to live is Christ and to die is gain" (1:21). You cannot live in two different directions. Jesus is asking you to choose. Are you willing to make that choice today and carry your cross?

THE PRAYER

Lord, the desires of our hearts lead us astray. They move us away from the plans and purposes You have for us. We surrender our own desires, and we pick up our cross so we can follow only You. Amen.

THE QUESTIONS

- Have you ever felt divided in what you desired and what you felt God desired for you? How did you handle the struggle?
- How do you know God has the best plan for your life?

Day 15
Combat the Enemy

JAMES 4:7-10 Submit yourselves, then, to God. Resist the devil, and he will flee from you. Come near to God and he will come near to you. Wash your hands, you sinners, and purify your hearts, you double-minded. Grieve, mourn and wail. Change your laughter to mourning and your joy to gloom. Humble yourselves before the Lord, and he will lift you up.

CONSIDER THIS

Don't judge me, but the mental picture I get when I read verse 7 is an old commercial for Raid Ant and Roach spray. I used to watch a lot of TV in the eighties and I remember one where the can of spray transformed into a superhero figure who pointed his finger at the "enemy" and as they were zapped, the bugs would run away in fear. Now, wouldn't it be nice if fighting the enemy was that easy? Just point your finger and no more conflict, no more temptation, no more struggles. At times it feels like the world is infested with temptation.

In his letter, James confronts believers, pointing to the way they have chosen to live by the whims of the world rather than the Word of God, being quick in their anger, playing favorites, speaking unkindly, and withholding their service to others. These believers wanted to control their choices and the consequences. In short, they wanted to have their cake and eat it too. We see this in verse 4, "You adulterous people, don't you know that friendship with the world means enmity against God?" But how could they find their way back to God? The answer was to surrender control and commit to God. And the good news is that James tells them because of God's grace, no matter how far they had gone, they could find their way back!

When you started this Lenten journey and began seeking out a space to encounter God, did you find it hard to embrace surrender? If you did, trust me, you are not alone. I love that James said to resist the enemy. Did you notice that he did not suggest we run away and hide or pretend the enemy doesn't exist? Instead, he chose language with military imagery, the picture of an army arranging themselves to oppose their enemy face-to-face. That's why it is called spiritual warfare! This is our position. Intentional and head-on.

But resist the devil? How do we fight what we cannot always see? The answer is submission. It might be surprising to you, but our power position is on our knees, not on our feet. Jonathan Edwards, a bold preacher during the first Great

Awakening, wrote, "Nothing sets a Christian so much out of the devil's reach than humility."[4] Surrendering is not a position of weakness, but it places us in a position to lean on the power of the Holy Spirit.

From this power position of surrender we can draw near to God. Remember that during Lent we want to face the mirror and assess the state of our lives so we can be altar'd. We need to ask ourselves, where have we chosen a life in the world rather than obedience to God? Where do we need to purify our hearts or refocus our minds? As we draw near to God through spiritual disciplines of prayer, study, worship, and confession, we will be able to resist the temptations that lurk in the corners of our lives. As we commit ourselves to the Lord, He will lift us up and bring us back into His presence.

THE PRAYER

Lord, help us stand ready. We know that we have not been obedient and we've allowed the enemy a foothold in our lives. We confess that we have followed the world rather than Your Word. Forgive us and help us fight the enemy. Amen.

---

4. Jonathan Edwards and Perry Miller, *The Works of Jonathan Edwards*, Christian Classics Ethereal Library (New Haven, CT: Yale University Press, 1957), Part IV, Section 1, 399. https://ccel.org/ccel/edwards/works1/works1.i.xiv.html.

THE QUESTIONS

- Do you find it helpful to envision the enemy as an army that we need to resist? If not, how do you view the enemy?
- In what ways do you find it hard to surrender control and submit to God?

Day 16

Recovering Perfectionist

JUDGES 6:12-14 When the angel of the Lord appeared to Gideon, he said, "The Lord is with you, mighty warrior."

"Pardon me, my lord," Gideon replied, "but if the Lord is with us, why has all this happened to us? Where are all his wonders that our ancestors told us about when they said, 'Did not the Lord bring us up out of Egypt?' But now the Lord has abandoned us and given us into the hand of Midian."

The Lord turned to him and said, "Go in the strength you have and save Israel out of Midian's hand. Am I not sending you?"

CONSIDER THIS

I have a chronic disease. It's the disease of wanting to be perfect. Whatever project I take on or job I have, this disease will rear its ugly head at some point and when it does, it can be debilitating, keeping me from moving forward. Surrendering control means believing in the call that God has given me.

In the book of Judges, Gideon is called by God to face the people who had kept the Israelites from flourishing. The Midianites had crushed their crops and bullied them into a place of fear. Gideon had two questions: Why were they suffering and what is God thinking? Gideon was from the weakest clan and he was the weakest in his family. Surely God had gotten the wrong Gideon. Maybe there was a Gideon in the next town who could be called mighty warrior, but surely God didn't mean him.

Remember that the purpose of the burnt offering was to express the total surrender of their obedience to the Lord, to not hold anything back. The Israelites had not been devoted to the one true God. They had worshipped other idols and disobeyed the Lord's commandments. Yet, in the face of their disobedience, God was still willing to save them from their suffering and the Lord would ask Gideon to fully surrender himself. "Am I not sending you?" God was not calling Gideon to fight the Midianites on his own, but to trust in the call of God on his life. Would he surrender himself fully?

If Gideon listened only to the voices in his head and contemplated the circumstances in front of him, he would never have stepped up to face the obstacle of the Midianites. But God loves imperfect people. God loves when we surrender our weaknesses to Him because it is in those moments we experience the miraculous power of the Lord in our lives. The Japanese art form of kintsugi is a visually beautiful illustration of God's perfection shining through our surrendered imperfections. Japanese artisans will take cracked pottery and fill the cracks with gold, not to hide the imperfections, but to celebrate that gold which makes it whole once again. God's call on Gideon's life and Gideon's surrender would allow the Lord to shine through him.

In response to God's promise to be with him, Gideon prepares an offering to the Lord which is wholly consumed by fire just like a burnt offering. In this encounter, he experiences the power of God through a supernatural peace and he names the altar, The Lord Is Peace. It is not through perfection that we find peace, but through surrendering our control to God's call on our life.

THE PRAYER

Lord, we know that we can only find peace by surrendering our plans to You. We commit ourselves to the call You have placed on our lives and believe that You are the one who equips us and sends us out for Your glory. Amen.

THE QUESTIONS

- When have you struggled with God's calling on your life? What has held you back from fully living into that call?
- How is Gideon's story an encouragement to lay down control and how will that change the way you live this week?

Day 17

Commit to the Next Generation

PSALM 78:1-6

My people, hear my teaching;
  listen to the words of my mouth.
I will open my mouth with a parable;
  I will utter hidden things, things from of old—
things we have heard and known,
  things our ancestors have told us.
We will not hide them from their descendants;
  we will tell the next generation
the praiseworthy deeds of the LORD,
  his power, and the wonders he has done.
He decreed statutes for Jacob
  and established the law in Israel,
which he commanded our ancestors
  to teach their children,
so the next generation would know them,
  even the children yet to be born,
  and they in turn would tell their children.

CONSIDER THIS

The season of Lent tends to have a vertical focus, meaning we spend a lot of time looking at our own relationship with the Lord. Where have we fallen short? Where can we become more disciplined and grow. But discipleship is both vertical and horizontal. It is about our relationship with the triune God and our relationship with others, so embracing a life of surrender means turning our eyes not just upward, but outward.

I love the Psalms. They are the heart-cries and the worship of God's children. This psalm was written by the great songwriter of David and Solomon's era, Asaph, who used his songs to teach the history of God and God's people not just for personal improvement, but to pass knowledge of God's story to the next generation. In today's passage, he reminds us that it is not only our obligation, but our privilege to tell our children and our children's children about God. And why wouldn't we? It's the greatest story ever told, isn't it? It's the foundation of our identity and the source of our hope. This is exactly what Moses told the people in Israel after they were freed from slavery to the Egyptians: "These commandments that I give you today are to be on your hearts. Impress them on your children. Talk about them when you sit at home and when you walk along the road, when you lie down and when you get up" (Deut. 6:6–7). Asaph reminds us that our parents, our ancestors, told us these things of God and we should not hide them from our children, our descendants.

Let's be honest, it doesn't always seem like our children want to listen. Maybe when they are little it was easier to get them to listen to the stories of Jesus and teach them about God, but as children grow up, how can we keep sharing God's story? This is where I remember that the author of the psalm, Asaph, was a singer. We know that our brains are wired in a way that allows us to recall information better when we hear it as music, which is why I can remember lyrics from a song in the '80s, but cannot remember what I read last week. It's the reason we sing songs to people with Alzheimer's because it is a powerful tool in cognitive therapy. Songs open the wellspring of our souls and our minds and help us remember!

A song is a powerful tool to tell the story of God. Just as Asaph wrote, the songs of God's people can tell the praiseworthy deeds of the Lord, His power, and the wonders He has done. Think of the great hymns of Charles Wesley like "O for a Thousand Tongues to Sing" and "Christ the Lord Is Risen Today." Did your brain start singing them? Of course, it did! We need to continue to share these hymns with our children, but do not dismiss the modern Christian singers and songwriters. Do not underestimate their ability to write new songs of God's story as a tool to share with the next generation. Even as God was laying the foundation of these devotionals on my heart, He was writing new songs about altars and surrender on the hearts of Bristol House, a worship movement that exists to carry on the heritage of the Wesleyan people and to share the story of God to all generations.[5] This is no coincidence! The Holy Spirit wants us to sing as a people of God!

Let us begin this Lenten season to commit to singing the songs of God and sharing them so our children and their children will know the greatest story ever told and the Holy Spirit will awaken the wellspring of their souls.

THE PRAYER

Lord, stir our hearts with Your songs, the ones that remind us of Your power and wonder. Open up new ways to share Your story with the next generation so that Your next great awakening may come through them. Amen.

THE QUESTIONS

- What is your favorite hymn? What story of God does it tell?
- How can music be a bridge between generations and in what ways can you use it to share the story of Christ's life and resurrection?

---

5. By the way, if you don't know about the Bristol House movement, connect with them at www.bristolhousemusic.org or on your favorite streaming platform.

Day 18
Who Is Will?

LUKE 22:39-42 Jesus went out as usual to the Mount of Olives, and his disciples followed him. On reaching the place, he said to them, "Pray that you will not fall into temptation." He withdrew about a stone's throw beyond them, knelt down and prayed, "Father, if you are willing, take this cup from me; yet not my will, but yours be done."

CONSIDER THIS

Not my will, but Your will. So, who is will? Yes, that is a joke, sorry. The passage we are meditating on today is likely very familiar to many of us. It is both comforting because we see Jesus struggle with a very human emotion and it is awe-inspiring because He surpasses the response most of us would have.

In terms of the Lenten story, we are jumping to the final days of Jesus's earthly ministry because we cannot speak of surrendering control without spending time studying Jesus's example. After He celebrates the Passover meal with His disciples, Jesus takes His inner circle of friends out of the city and into the garden of Gethsemane to pray. When Jesus chose the space He would use for prayer, He knelt down. It was the custom of the Jewish people to stand while praying, but Jesus would choose to place His body in a position of surrender, first on His knees and then on His face. As an offering on an altar is laid out in surrender, this was the position Jesus chose. The altar is Jesus Himself. It is in this sacred space that Jesus opens Himself to His Father and asks to be saved from the painful death He knows is coming.

As a believer, it is hard to surrender to the unknown, but it is even harder to surrender when we know the future will be painful. I think of Daniel in the Old Testament who knew that he would be thrown into a fire if he did not agree to worship the Babylonian king. I think of Stephen in the book of Acts who knew he would be killed if he continued to preach about Jesus. Surrendering control for total commitment means letting go of what we want in order to follow the path God has set in front of us.

I am grateful to see Jesus ask God to release Him from pain, yet in the same breath He shows His willingness to face what is ahead if it is God's will. Jesus provides for us, the most significant example of surrender: His life. His surrender would encompass His mind, body, and spirit. This was not Jesus's first time at the Mount of Olives, and it was not His first time to seek the presence of His Father in prayer. It takes effort to place ourselves in the garden with Jesus. The tenderness of His heart to call on God as Father and to clearly submit Himself—not once but twice—is truly painful. *Are You willing, Father, to keep Me from this ultimate sacrifice of My life? I am willing to be obedient and sacrifice My life for Your plan of salvation.* Was it the regular act of obedience that made the words "not my will but yours" come out of His mouth more easily? Jesus had surrendered Himself in prayer many times throughout His ministry, but this would be the final altar and the ultimate example for us to follow.

THE PRAYER

Lord, today we pray the prayer You taught Your disciples to pray. "Our Father in heaven, hallowed be your name, your kingdom come, your will be done, on earth as it is in heaven. Give us today our daily bread. And forgive us our debts, as we also have forgiven our debtors. And lead us not into temptation, but deliver us from the evil one, for yours is the kingdom and the power and the glory forever" (Matt. 6:9–13).

THE QUESTIONS

- When have you been tempted to follow your own plans instead of seeking God's plan?
- Why do you think Jesus chose to kneel instead of following the custom of standing to pray?
- With what area of your life have you not surrendered to God's will?

Part Three

Surrender Worry for Trust (Grain Offering)

Day 19
First and Foremost

LEVITICUS 2:1-3 "When anyone brings a grain offering to the LORD, their offering is to be of the finest flour. They are to pour olive oil on it, put incense on it and take it to Aaron's sons the priests. The priest shall take a handful of the flour and oil, together with all the incense, and burn this as a memorial portion on the altar, a food offering, an aroma pleasing to the LORD. The rest of the grain offering belongs to Aaron and his sons; it is a most holy part of the food offerings presented to the LORD."

CONSIDER THIS

This is a new week and we are embracing the surrender of worry. If the reports from mental health experts are correct, this is desperately needed by a growing number of adults, especially our young adults. Worry seems to be an invisible burden many of us carry on a daily basis. Why do we worry? Do we not trust in God's goodness or believe we deserve God's provision? This week we will face some common worries like not having enough or not having *anything*, worries about not *being* enough, not knowing our future, and not being able to let go of all our worries. Whatever the root cause of this mental weight, God has invited us to surrender our worry in exchange for trust in His unfailing love.

In Leviticus, the second type of offering God directed His people to give was a grain offering, or the *minchah*. Interestingly, it is the only offering that did not involve an animal sacrifice though it often accompanied a burnt offering we studied last week. Why grain? As you read stories in the Old Testament, you will find that bread was a fundamental piece of their diet. Whether rich or poor, having flour and oil to make bread was essential to living and it was a common bond between all people. This offering also provided for the priests. While the burnt offering was wholly consumed, part of the grain offering was meant to support those who served God. There are two words that rise up (yes, baking humor) from today's passage, *anyone* and *finest*.

One of my favorite parts of Communion liturgy in the Wesleyan expression occurs when the pastor provides the invitation, reminding those who have gathered that the altar is an open table and all are welcome to come and receive, you need only have a repentant heart. Both in this offering lesson and our Communion liturgy is the word *anyone*. Whether you are rich or poor, well-connected or lonely, of the highest heritage or lowest, you are invited to encounter God. We do not have to worry if we measure up or if the Lord will accept us. He desires all to come into His presence.

The second word is *finest*. Just as the burnt offering was to be of highest value, the grain was expected to be the best or the finest. The grain offering is also known as a "firstfruits" offering. In Genesis 4 we can read the story of Cain and Abel bringing their offerings to God. Abel brought the firstfruits of his livestock, but Cain's offering from his garden was not the finest. It caused God to be angry and resulted in fatal conflict between the brothers. We do not have to hold back our best from God because He does not hold back from us. Instead, we can trust God to provide because the Lord is good and faithful. Are you carrying the invisible burden of worry today? We can trust who we are and what we have to the Lord who loves us and who promises to be our provider.

THE PRAYER

Lord, we want to give You our first and our finest. You are worthy of more than we can give, so we give You our best and pray that You will use it for Your kingdom. Amen.

THE QUESTIONS

- Do you worry more about who you are or what you have? Why is that your worry?
- Where have you failed to give the firstfruits of your life and your resources?

Day 20

A Fork in the Road

1 KINGS 18:21-22, 30-39 Elijah went before the people and said, "How long will you waver between two opinions? If the Lᴏʀᴅ is God, follow him; but if Baal is God, follow him."

But the people said nothing.

Then Elijah said to them, "I am the only one of the Lᴏʀᴅ's prophets left, but Baal has four hundred and fifty prophets." . . .

Then Elijah said to all the people, "Come here to me." They came to him, and he repaired the altar of the Lᴏʀᴅ, which had been torn down. Elijah took twelve stones, one for each of the tribes descended from Jacob, to whom the word of the Lᴏʀᴅ had come, saying, "Your name shall be Israel." With the stones he built an altar in the name of the Lᴏʀᴅ, and he dug a trench around it large enough to hold two seahs of seed. He arranged the wood, cut the bull into pieces and laid it on the wood. Then he said to them, "Fill four large jars with water and pour it on the offering and on the wood."

"Do it again," he said, and they did it again.

"Do it a third time," he ordered, and they did it the third time. The water ran down around the altar and even filled the trench.

At the time of sacrifice, the prophet Elijah stepped forward and prayed: "LORD, the God of Abraham, Isaac and Israel, let it be known today that you are God in Israel and that I am your servant and have done all these things at your command. Answer me, LORD, answer me, so these people will know that you, LORD, are God, and that you are turning their hearts back again."

Then the fire of the LORD fell and burned up the sacrifice, the wood, the stones and the soil, and also licked up the water in the trench.

When all the people saw this, they fell prostrate and cried, "The LORD—he is God! The LORD—he is God!"

CONSIDER THIS

In Elijah's altar story, he is called to not only draw God's people back to faithfulness, but he also has to confront an evil king. As a prophet, Elijah had to stand up against opposition, and in this conflict we learn the power of surrendering worry. In the book of 1 Kings, the prophet Elijah had a calling from God to speak against the unfaithful and idolatrous King Ahab so he set up a challenge. Ahab had built altars to the idol Baal and Scriptures describe him as doing "more evil in the eyes of the LORD than any of those before him" (1 Kings 16:30). At the same time, the Israelite people had become afraid and failed to stay faithful to God allowing the Lord's altars to become torn down. However, Elijah, even in the face of a king who wanted to kill him, trusted God, had the courage to believe in His power, and created a head-to-head competition with Baal. After Elijah restored the Lord's altar, he threw down the challenge flag and offered Ahab's team a handicap to make it more interesting by pouring water on the wood for the Lord's altar. Despite the added barriers, the Lord proved Himself worthy of their trust as He consumed the sacrifice.

This was a long passage but place yourself in the story. If you had been Elijah, would you have worried? Would you have been concerned about the outcome and what everyone would think if God didn't come through? How did Elijah surrender the temptation to worry and lean into the trust he had in God? Worry manifests when we play out the negative *potential* outcomes in our minds. When we worry, we forget about God's past provisions and His past victories. When we worry, we allow the enemy to convince us that God is not true to His character, that He is not faithful or able to direct our future. When we surrender our worry, we can be like Elijah who believed God did it before and He can do it again.

Why do you think Elijah called all the people to watch what would happen? I believe it was because Elijah knew the people were carrying an invisible burden of worry. They had become unfaithful in their devotion to God and had been swept up by the idolatrous culture. The farther they went from God, the greater the pull of the enemy. Elijah knew their hearts and knew that God wanted to draw them back to Himself. Elijah trusted God to act because he had seen the miracles of God in the past.

In the same way, Jesus knows the worries we carry in our hearts today. He sees us being swept up by a culture that tells us we have to rely only on ourselves because the world is crumbling around us. He knows that we have short memories for the blessings we have been given and the ways we've seen God at work in our lives. Jesus reminded the disciples who had been witness to many miracles and walked closely with Him, "Let not your hearts be troubled. You believe in God, believe also in me" (John 14:1). Perhaps that is our goal today, to reflect on the troubles of our heart. I believe God wants to turn your heart back to Him today by reminding you of what He has done. Where have you seen God's faithfulness before? Can you lay down your worries today because of God's goodness in the past?

THE PRAYER

Lord, we know we do not have to worry about the outcome of anything You call us to, we only need to be obedient. Let our trust in You lead us to be bold witnesses so others can experience You. Amen.

THE QUESTIONS

- What is your biggest worry right now?
- In your prayer time today, say aloud the words, "The Lord—He is God!"

Day 21

Best Thing Since Sliced …

JOHN 6:47-51 "Very truly I tell you, the one who believes has eternal life. I am the bread of life. Your ancestors ate the manna in the wilderness, yet they died. But here is the bread that comes down from heaven, which anyone may eat and not die. I am the living bread that came down from heaven. Whoever eats this bread will live forever. This bread is my flesh, which I will give for the life of the world."

CONSIDER THIS

What is the best idea you've ever heard? Apparently, in 1928, the Chillicothe Baking Company had a great idea and they became the first company to sell sliced bread. Afterward people used this moment as a benchmark and a way to denote a great idea or innovation. As much as I appreciate this improvement in the world, I am confident in saying that Jesus is the best thing since *before* sliced bread!

When we began this week, we learned that grain was essential to the daily life of the Israelites. It was the center of their existence. Without bread, many of them would not be able to survive. While I would venture to guess that most of us do not worry about surviving each day, what do you believe you need in your life? What is essential for your daily life? Psychologist Abraham Maslow created a list of needs every human being has from those essentials to security, belonging, esteem, and purpose. Many of us tend to worry because we have our own list of what we need to be satisfied. We worry because we don't believe God will provide enough of what we have decided we need. That's a key word: *enough*. Will we have enough? We are worried because we believe we'll end up with the least, but the truth is we can trust Jesus because He is not only enough, He is the best.

In the Gospel of John, Jesus fed more than five thousand people by multiplying bread. He took the bare essentials of a few loaves and fish and He provided all they needed plus baskets of leftovers. The next day the crowd went in search for Jesus on the other side of the lake and they have asked Him for a sign like the manna which was given to their ancestors in the desert. Jesus responds that He is the bread they need, but it is more than the bare minimum essentials. Jesus is enough because He is the best and He can multiply all things to be not only enough, but to be overflowing.

Is there an area in your life where you do not feel you have enough physically? Maybe it's money or a job or a home. Is there a place in your spiritual life where you do not feel you have enough knowledge of the Bible or experience in prayer? Surrender your worry to Jesus Christ, the Bread of Life and the Creator of all. We do not have to worry that God is not enough for our lives. He is all we need.

THE PRAYER

Lord, why do we worry? You are everything we need. You are the one who knows how to provide, so today we lay down our fish and our bread, we surrender all we have and we trust You to be all we need. Amen.

THE QUESTIONS

- Why do you think Jesus made a point of stressing that, like manna, He came down from heaven? How does that increase your trust in God?
- What does it mean to you that Jesus is the best and most important need we have? How will you re-prioritize the list of needs you have in your mind?

Day 22

Who's on First?

MATTHEW 6:33-34 "But seek first his kingdom and his righteousness, and all these things will be given to you as well. Therefore do not worry about tomorrow, for tomorrow will worry about itself. Each day has enough trouble of its own."

CONSIDER THIS

In the 1930s, the famous comedian duo Abbott and Costello entertained audiences with a sketch called, "Who's on First?" It's a funny example of miscommunication, but it's also a great question to ask ourselves. In your life, who's on first? When you wake up, what first comes to your mind? Do your worries come first or your blessings? What do you fill your mind with first? The world news? Social media? Scripture? Let me ask you again, do your worries come first to your mind or your blessings?

At the beginning of the week we learned that the grain offering is also referred to as the offering of firstfruits. In our Matthew passage today, Jesus is teaching the gathered crowd who is to be first in their lives and what should be of first importance. Prior to this passage Jesus told them not to store up their treasures on earth, but to put the kingdom of God first. This does not mean that God will give earthly riches, but it will mean that their trust won't be found in those earthly riches. If they seek the kingdom first, their minds won't be consumed by the anxieties of the world.

Let's think again about our mornings and who is on first. Jesus tells us that if we seek first the news of the world, our minds will focus on the turbulent waters of politics and the economy. If we seek first the social media posts of our friends, our minds will focus on what other people have or have done. But if we seek first the kingdom and His righteousness, our minds will be grounded in the promises of our Savior.

It doesn't mean we won't have trouble. For years, when I read these verses, my brain focused on three little words, "do not worry." I'm not sure I even paid attention to the rest of the verse. Those three simple words form a wonderful platitude and would look good on someone's car as a bumper sticker, but living that reality is not as simple as the words themselves. As I studied this passage again, this time my brain focused on the end of the sentence. Each day has trouble. Wait, what? That is not very reassuring. I thought I wasn't supposed to worry. If I am honest, "each day will have enough trouble" feels much more relatable to my present reality. I may not look at the news or social media first, but the reality of the world is that there are troubles, fluctuating interest rates, the price of gasoline, escalating violence, wildfires and floods, and starving children around the world. How can I surrender worry about these realities? This answer is because the Lord's provision is not limited. You will not use up all His provision today, so you do not have to worry about tomorrow. He is enough for today and He will be enough for tomorrow.

While Jesus did not promise a trouble-free life, He does promise daily bread and daily grace. We do not have to worry about tomorrow and because of His faithfulness, we do not have to worry about today either. Let's encourage one another to start each day creating space to encounter God. Let us lay down our worries for today and not borrow from tomorrow. In place of our worry, let us lean into the trust that through His righteousness we live in the kingdom promise today!

Meditate on the words of the hymn, "I Surrender All."

All to Jesus I surrender
All to Him I freely give
I will ever love and trust Him
In His presence daily live.

THE PRAYER

Lord, how many times do we need to read this passage to remember to put You first in our minds and in our hearts? We choose You first today. We seek You and only You today.

We trust You for today and tomorrow we will trust You again. Amen.

THE QUESTIONS

- What is the first thing you look at each morning? How does that direct what your mind focuses on for the day?
- What are you worried about today? Are you willing to lay it down and trust God in that circumstance?

Day 23
Enough

2 CORINTHIANS 12:9-10 But he said to me, "My grace is sufficient for you, for my power is made perfect in weakness." Therefore, I will boast all the more gladly about my weaknesses, so that Christ's power may rest on me. That is why, for Christ's sake, I delight in weaknesses, in insults, in hardships, in persecutions, in difficulties. For when I am weak, then I am strong.

CONSIDER THIS

Am I enough? That's a question that plagues me and I know I'm not the only one. Late one night I was mindlessly scrolling through social media as the worries in my heart and mind were spinning at a frenzied pace. Yes, I know that's not a good way to spend my time and I don't recommend it. But it was as if the advertising fairies could see into my soul and knew the burden I was carrying because at that moment, an ad popped up for a sweatshirt that caught my eye and caused me to stop scrolling. On the back were these words, "Dear person behind me, the world is a better place with you in it. Love, the person in front of you." I could imagine myself walking along a sidewalk or hallway, coming up behind this person and believing that God had directed me to see it as a sign from Him. I needed that message.

We all have weaknesses, and they feel like neon signs hovering over us, pointing down and telling everyone why we're not good enough and where we are failing. And yet, Jesus doesn't care what your neon signs say, in fact, I don't think He even sees the signs. When Paul wrote these words to the Corinthians, he wasn't trying to hide his weaknesses. He was boasting about them! He had been given a "thorn" in his flesh which tormented him. In his culture, physical ailments were often viewed as signs of sin and were causes for shame and embarrassment. We don't know what that thorn was and I don't believe we're meant to know because we all carry some thorn in our lives. Are you thinking about yours right now?

Paul didn't want the thorn and he begged the Lord to take it away, but for reasons known only to God, His answer to Paul was no. So instead of pity or bitterness that God wouldn't answer his prayer, Paul turned the tables on the thorn and decided to boast about it. Why would he boast? So that Christ's power might rest on him. In the Amplified Bible, we read, "Therefore, I will all the more gladly boast in my weaknesses, so that the power of Christ [may completely enfold me and] may dwell in me." Paul knew that his weaknesses would not limit his witness, but it was the weakness itself that would be the sign of God's power.

If you are tired of trying to be smart enough, talented enough, strong enough, successful enough, or worthy enough, remember that the power of the Holy Spirit dwells in you because you are a child of the Most High King and it is not your weakness that defines you, but the one who dwells inside of you. And yes, I did buy that sweatshirt from social media and when I look at the mirror, I see the words that are written on the front, "You are enough."

THE PRAYER

Lord, thank You that we don't have to be enough, because You are enough. For those of us who are weighed down by our weaknesses today, remind us that it is Your power and Your presence that makes us enough. Amen.

THE QUESTIONS

- When have you felt like you were not enough? What promises from Scripture encouraged you?
- How can the promise of the Lord's presence give you boldness to face a worry that you need to surrender?

Day 24

Blind Faith

GENESIS 12:1-2 The LORD said to Abram, "Go from your country and your kindred and your father's house to the land that I will show you.

"I will make you into a great nation,
and I will bless you;
I will make your name great,
and you will be a blessing."

CONSIDER THIS

Before I became a Christian, it seemed that most people who talked about "following God" described some sort of blind faith. Like using a divining rod or rolling the dice to see how far they should move, following the Christian faith seemed disconcerting. Does your faith feel blind sometimes? We are about halfway through this Lenten season, intentionally creating space to encounter the triune God and voluntarily surrendering our lives as an offering to the Lord. Are you experiencing a shift or transformation in your spiritual life? I pray that you are because as you put these steps into practice you will better understand that following Jesus is not blind. As we learn to listen to the Holy Spirit, it is easier to follow God's direction and as we read today, following God leads to blessings.

In a pivotal moment of Abram's (soon to be Abraham's) life, he hears the Lord tell him to go to a new place so He can bless him—in that call, the Lord is asking him to trust God with his future. Why didn't the Lord just bless Abram where he was? Why did Abram have to pick up his household and move to another location? The truth is sometimes we need a physical shift to experience a spiritual shift. We have to let go of our lives to receive a blessing from the Lord.

In reality, God could have blessed Abram in any location and in any circumstances, but God wanted Abram to be the vessel through which He would bless the world and that would require trust. God didn't need his possessions or even his location. God needed his obedience. In the ancient world, your land was your inheritance to pass on to your children and to provide and protect your household. Abram's call to obedience meant that he had to put everything into God's hand and trust Him with his future. He would hold nothing back. In fact, if you continue in chapter 12, you see that he took everything, "He took his wife Sarai, his nephew Lot, all the possessions they had accumulated and the people they had acquired in Harran" (v. 5). He didn't leave some clothes in the closet just in case or put his house up for rent so he would have a place to return to if God's plan didn't work out.

As a sign of trust, Abram left what was comfortable and what was known, to go where God directed.

The disciples were given a similar directive when Jesus said, "Follow me." They had to lay down any worry they had about their new profession, how they would provide for themselves and their families, and where they were going. Following your faith in Jesus can bring you to a crossroads in your life. Will you stay in the place where you know everything and everyone or will you go to a new place? Are you willing to physically shift to experience a spiritual shift? While it may seem that the first step of Abram's surrender started with his feet, it actually began with his relationship with God. Did he trust in the voice of the Lord? Did he trust in the plans the Lord had for him? The answer is yes and so can we!

THE PRAYER

Lord, we may not know what the future holds, but You do. We trust You with our days and we will go where You tell us to go without reservation. Amen.

THE QUESTIONS

- When have you felt God direct you to make a change in your life? Did you struggle with any doubt or were you confident in the change?
- How does your relationship with Jesus help you when you find yourself at a crossroads?

Day 25

We're All in This Together

1 PETER 5:6-10 Humble yourselves, therefore, under God's mighty hand, that he may lift you up in due time. Cast all your anxiety on him because he cares for you.

Be alert and of sober mind. Your enemy the devil prowls around like a roaring lion looking for someone to devour. Resist him, standing firm in the faith, because you know that the family of believers throughout the world is undergoing the same kind of sufferings.

And the God of all grace, who called you to his eternal glory in Christ, after you have suffered a little while, will himself restore you and make you strong, firm and steadfast.

CONSIDER THIS

In Peter's letter to other believers, he doesn't promise that God will lift them up the moment their knees hit the ground, but by humbling ourselves, surrendering to God, they will be restored even if they have to suffer for a little while. Suffering is not a new concept for us as believers and it is affirmed throughout Scriptures, but we are not to fear suffering. We are to embrace it, just as we embrace surrender.

We cannot surrender if we do not learn humility and Peter tells us how to be humble, it is by casting our worries onto Jesus. Peter's life as a disciple was filled, literally, with highs and lows. He stood on the top of the mountain as Jesus was transfigured and God's glory shone all around. He also hid in the darkness after he denied Jesus three times. Peter knew suffering. He also knew worry, but in this letter, he offers encouragement and support to other followers of Jesus. He tells them to cast their anxiety, not just the heavy burdens or the worries that seem impossible to fix themselves, not just one or two worries, but all of their worries. Today our challenge is not to embrace the worries, but to embrace letting them all go.

Again, sometimes words seem so simple, but the actions are so difficult. As a fisherman, Peter chose this term, *cast*, which provides an image for us. If you've seen a photo of the nets they used in the time of Jesus, you would know that these nets were not like the fishing rods we have today. The net was round with weights on the outside so as it was thrown, the net would spread out like a parachute and the weights would cause it to sink quickly in the water. Take this image and mentally cast your worries out to Jesus. Imagine them spreading out and then sinking into the water. Watch them drop below the surface out of sight.

There are two pieces of good news the Lord promises as He exchanges humility for hope. First, He will restore us and make us strong, firm, and steadfast. As we share in Christ's suffering, we will also be restored in His character. Second, we are all in this together. As believers, we do not suffer alone and we do not have to carry the burden of surrender alone. Look around in your church and your friend group. If you have a covenant community, they are God's gift to you so we can suffer and be restored together. If you do not yet have a covenant community, start a discipleship band because we are not meant to walk this journey alone (discipleshipbands.com).

THE PRAYER

Lord, thank You for being strong enough and willing to receive every burden we carry. For those of us suffering under the weight today, I pray that You will give us the courage to cast every worry on You so we can feel the burden lifted. Amen.

THE QUESTIONS

- Are you holding back from surrendering some worries because they feel too small or you want to handle yourself? If so, lay them down now.
- How has the suffering from your past affected the worry you are carrying right now?

Part Four

Surrender Thanks for Peace (Peace Offering)

Day 26
If

LEVITICUS 3:1-2 "If your offering is a fellow-ship offering, and you offer an animal from the herd, whether male or female, you are to present before the LORD an animal without defect. You are to lay your hand on the head of your offering and slaughter it at the entrance to the tent of meeting. Then Aaron's sons the priests shall splash the blood against the sides of the altar."

CONSIDER THIS

The word *if* is incredibly small, but it has great consequences. *If* places you at a fork in the road where you have a choice to make. *If* allows you to choose the posture of your heart and the trajectory of your future. Wow, that is a lot of power in a small package, but it is an important word for us this week as we focus on surrendering our thanks. Yes, you read that correctly. As we start a new week in Lent, we are surrendering our gratitude and thanksgiving as we ask the Lord to transform us into His image.

The third offering the Lord teaches the Israelites is known as the peace offering or the fellowship offering because in the Hebrew, the word for this offering is *selemim,* which has a root connection to the Hebrew word *shalom* or *peace* and it can also mean a vow. This offering was brought as a celebration of God's faithfulness for answered prayers and it was often part of a community celebration meal because only a small portion of the animal was placed on the altar while the rest of the animal was shared with family and friends.

But let's return to this small word *if.* The peace offering was optional. It was not part of the daily sacrifices made at the temple but was given as a freewill offering or to fulfill a vow. The Lord did not require it, but He desired it. He wanted His children to hit the pause button in their lives to acknowledge His gifts; He wanted the community to share these moments of joy and answered prayers with other believers.

But how can an optional offering of thanks be important to our journey this Lent? Let me ask, have you ever watched a child being given a gift? After they tear into the package and pull out of the box the glorious toy they have been asking for, what happens? Typically, you hear the parent whisper, "What do you say?" and then the child says thank you as the joy spreads across their face! At the same time, everyone else gathered in that room smiles or cheers because they have witnessed a beautiful exchange of appreciation. And every parent hopes that after a few years or a few holidays, the child will respond without prompting because he has developed a habit of giving thanks.

This habit changes us. We develop an attitude of gratitude. This week, our offering and altar story will help us learn how to surrender our thanks and gain peace. Embracing the surrender of thanks must be done in all circumstance; it has a cost, marks a covenant, commends, and celebrates despite the chaos of life. All of this happens if we choose to offer the Lord our thanks as a peace offering. Get ready to give some thanks and praise this week!

THE PRAYER

Lord, it seems only right that we begin with praise. Thank You for this Lenten journey and the opportunity we have been given to study Your Word, to be expectant for the Holy Spirit to transform us, and the joy of sharing this season with others. Thank You, Jesus! Amen.

THE QUESTIONS

- What can you thank God for today?
- What is something God has provided for you when you did not stop and give Him the gratitude He deserved?

Day 27

Marking the Moments

JOSHUA 8:30-35 Then Joshua built on Mount Ebal an altar to the Lord, the God of Israel, as Moses the servant of the Lord had commanded the Israelites. He built it according to what is written in the Book of the Law of Moses—an altar of uncut stones, on which no iron tool had been used. On it they offered to the Lord burnt offerings and sacrificed fellowship offerings. There, in the presence of the Israelites, Joshua wrote on stones a copy of the law of Moses. All the Israelites, with their elders, officials and judges, were standing on both sides of the ark of the covenant of the Lord, facing the Levitical priests who carried it. Both the foreigners living among them and the native-born were there. Half of the people stood in front of Mount Gerizim and half of them in front of Mount Ebal, as Moses the servant of the Lord had formerly commanded when he gave instructions to bless the people of Israel.

Afterward, Joshua read all the words of the law—the blessings and the curses—just as it is written in the Book of the Law. There was not a word of all that Moses had commanded that Joshua did not

read to the whole assembly of Israel, including the
women and children, and the foreigners who lived
among them.

CONSIDER THIS

True confession: I am not the best at marking the important moments of life. Many of us probably grew up creating
scrapbooks or physical photo albums to mark a special vaca-
tion or a pivotal year of a life. With technology, it has become
even easier (at least for some) to create digital albums
or scrolling photo frames to celebrate those milestone
moments. And yet, even with the help of technology, some
of us (yes, me) have missed the opportunity to commemo-
rate an important time.

In our altar story, we find Joshua, the leader of the
Israelites, stopping to mark a moment and give thanks to God
rather than continuing to battle. Joshua had succeeded Moses
and moved everyone into the promised land. They had fought
the battle of Jericho and Ai and now with the momentum
of success, Joshua takes a very unusual military tactic. He
stops. Instead of pushing ahead to gain the upper hand in his
next battle, he stops to give thanks to God. Joshua marks the
moment. He builds an altar in the manner God had directed
Moses. He offered sacrifices to the Lord, read the Word of
God aloud, and inscribed the law on the stones. Joshua marks

the moment and makes a clear connection that any success they have experienced is tied to God's covenant promise.

It was important to Joshua that they did not forget that God was the one who was making the way through the promised land. It was because of God's power and His presence that they would see God's covenant fulfilled and he wanted to create space to remember where they had experienced God. Abraham had also used altars to mark moments of encounter.

> The LORD appeared to Abram and said, "To your offspring I will give this land." So he built an altar there to the LORD, who had appeared to him. From there he went on toward the hills east of Bethel and pitched his tent, with Bethel on the west and Ai on the east. There he built an altar to the LORD and called on the name of the LORD. (Gen. 12:7-8)

It takes time to mark these moments. To stop and surrender our time. How easy is it to work hard, keep our focus on the tasks ahead, receive recognition for our work, and forget to give thanks. Yet we are supposed to take a position of gratitude as a surrender of thanks not only because it honors God, but it sends a message to others. In verse 33 we see that foreigners and the native-born were part of the moment. They were a witness to the honor Jacob gave the Lord and they heard the Word read. It's like inviting the neighbors to an anniversary party. *Come and learn about our*

family and the Lord who has given us the greatest gift. Help us
mark the moment by giving our thanks. Let us praise not only the
gift, but also the Giver.

THE PRAYER

Almighty God, do not let us race through our lives and forget to stop and give thanks. May Your words be on our lips and our hearts sing Your praise. We know that all good things come from You and we do not want to take those gifts for granted. Thank You for moments to stop today. Amen.

THE QUESTIONS

- What is a moment in your faith journey you want to mark by thanking God?
- Why is it important to go back to the basics of our faith by remembering God's words? How does it help you to reset and prepare to move forward?

Day 28
Just Because

1 THESSALONIANS 5:16-18 Rejoice always, pray continually, give thanks in all circumstances; for this is God's will for you in Christ Jesus.

CONSIDER THIS

I'm not a huge fan of all the Hallmark holidays that fill our calendars. It seems that those days are filled with obligations and preconceived notions of the correct way to celebrate. Perhaps they are not my favorite because they also seem to be tied to a coincidental and temporary increase in the price of flowers or candy or whatever else we're supposed to buy for the one we love (yes, there is sarcasm in my voice). However, my favorite holiday is the "just because" day. You won't find it on any Hallmark list, but if you want to make me happy, bring me flowers on a random Tuesday just because. Or perhaps take me to brunch after church just because. Or you can even drop a card in the mail for no reason other than to say hello. The reason I love a just because gift is because of where it comes from. When we give a gift just because, it is one that bubbles up from a place of deep gratitude and not forced and it tells me how you really feel. When we give for *no* reason, it is because we know the *real* reason.

Rejoice always. I feel confident in guessing that you may not always feel like rejoicing. Is Paul saying that Christians are always supposed to be happy and walk around with rose-colored glasses? Maybe the question we should be asking is what we are using to determine our happiness. Is it our ever-changing circumstances or is it the ever-present love of Christ? When we only mark moments that have no pain or no challenges, we can train ourselves to think that there is a cause and effect when it comes to giving thanks. But in our lives, we need to remember to give thanks always.

In my home, I try to remember to thank my husband and my children when they do things to help out, especially if it's a task that I typically handle. But if I only give them thanks when they do something for me, they might think they have to earn my love. If I only give them thanks when I am pleased with them, they might think that when I am disappointed, I no longer love them. But I rejoice because of who they are, not just what they do for me. So yes, sometimes I have to surrender a thank you when I would rather grumble, but it is through the thank you they know I love them just because.

Pray continually. In his writings, the renowned preacher Charles Spurgeon said, "When joy and prayer are married their first-born child is gratitude."[6] Thankfulness is a recurring theme throughout the Bible from the prophets to the kings to the disciples who wanted to pray like Jesus. In the Psalms, David wrote, "I will bless the LORD at all times; his praise will always be in my mouth" (34:1 CEB).

This is God's will for us. The Lord knows that gratitude changes us. Being thankful in all circumstances teaches us to have a grateful heart. It teaches us to look for the good in our lives and in other people. It creates in us a heart of compassion and love like Jesus. When we choose to be thankful, we choose to show our devotion to God for *no* reason because we *know* the reason.

THE PRAYER

Lord, we give You our praise today, not because of our circumstances, but perhaps in spite of them. Thank You for loving us not because of what we can do for You, but because You simply love us. Help us love others in the same way. Amen.

THE QUESTIONS

- In what ways have your circumstances affected your ability to rejoice and give thanks to God?

---

6. "Pray Without Ceasing," The Spurgeon Center, March 10, 1872. https://www.spurgeon.org/resource-library/sermons/pray -without-ceasing.

- How can you give thanks to someone else just because this week?
- Why do you think God's will would include giving thanks, and how will that change the way you live this week?

Day 29

Busy Bees

LUKE 7:36-38 When one of the Pharisees invited Jesus to have dinner with him, he went to the Pharisee's house and reclined at the table. A woman in that town who lived a sinful life learned that Jesus was eating at the Pharisee's house, so she came there with an alabaster jar of perfume. As she stood behind him at his feet weeping, she began to wet his feet with her tears. Then she wiped them with her hair, kissed them and poured perfume on them.

CONSIDER THIS

Raise your hand if you consider your life busy. My guess is that a fair number of us had a hand in the air. Did you know that one of the challenges to surrendering our thanks is busyness? In his book *The Power of Human*, author Adam Waytz recounts an anecdote about a man who immigrated to the United States. As he learned the culture and the language, he came to believe that the word "busy" meant "good" because when he asked people how they were doing, they often responded with one word: "busy." Being a North American, I can attest to the cultural pressure that exists to climb the corporate ladder, accumulate wealth, have your kids succeed in afterschool activities, and constantly be on the go. The unspoken value of busyness is everywhere. By the way, none of those activities I just mentioned are, on their own, bad. However, if your busyness keeps you from slowing down and offering your thanks, then you are missing an encounter with the Lord and surrendering our thanks has a cost.

In Luke's Gospel we read the story of a woman who brought to Jesus a jar of expensive perfume which she broke open and poured out on Him. We could take a deep theological dive into these few verses as there is much to learn, but today I want to encourage you to see this as a *selemim* offering. She did not have to give it, but she made a choice. She did not give from obligation, but an open heart. She did not come for an hour, put her offering in a basket, and immediately leave to go back to her daily activities. Just like Joshua did in yesterday's story, she stopped. She wasn't too busy or distracted by the world to surrender her thanksgiving and linger with her Savior as an act of worship. This outpouring of her time cost her, but it would be repaid by an outpouring of mercy and peace from Jesus.

There are many contrasts in the passage. The Pharisees were religious and educated. The woman was sinful and wasn't allowed to study. The Pharisees were there to question Jesus. The woman was there to worship Jesus. The Pharisees were prideful. The woman was humble. The Pharisee shunned the sinful woman. Jesus showed her mercy. Because the woman was willing to come before Jesus with her broken offering, she received wholeness and redemption. What a moment.

I love that the gift she offered was viewed as expensive and extravagant, but the reality is, it would not have mattered to Jesus the cost of the gift. In Mark's Gospel we read, "Many rich people threw in large amounts. But a poor widow came and put in two very small copper coins, worth only a few cents. Calling his disciples to him, Jesus said, 'Truly I tell you, this poor widow has put more into the treasury than all the others'" (12:41–43). He gave praise to the widow who offered her two small copper coins because both gifts were given from a heart of joy and gratitude. In exchange for their surrender and obedience, Jesus offers peace. "Peace I leave with you; my peace I give you. I do not give to you as the world gives. Do not let your hearts be troubled and do not be afraid" (John 14:27). This is the same peace He offers to you today. Let us respond to the extravagant grace of Jesus by slowing down, perhaps even stopping, and pour out our thanks to the one who has poured out Himself for us.

THE PRAYER

Lord, what could we give to show our gratitude for Your love? Today, we don't want to hold anything back from You. We give You all of ourselves. Amen.

THE QUESTIONS

- In what ways have you allowed busyness to get in the way of giving thanks to God?
- If you were to sit at the feet of Jesus today, what are some of the things for which you would thank Him?

Day 30
Solemn Vow

1 SAMUEL 1:10-11, 24-28 In her deep anguish Hannah prayed to the LORD, weeping bitterly. And she made a vow, saying, "LORD Almighty, if you will only look on your servant's misery and remember me, and not forget your servant but give her a son, then I will give him to the LORD for all the days of his life, and no razor will ever be used on his head." . . .

After he was weaned, she took the boy with her, young as he was, along with a three-year-old bull, an ephah of flour and a skin of wine, and brought him to the house of the LORD at Shiloh. When the bull had been sacrificed, they brought the boy to Eli, and she said to him, "Pardon me, my lord. As surely as you live, I am the woman who stood here beside you praying to the LORD. I prayed for this child, and the LORD has granted me what I asked of him. So now I give him to the LORD. For his whole life he will be given over to the LORD." And he worshiped the LORD there.

CONSIDER THIS

When I officiate a wedding, one of the sweetest moments is the moment the bride and groom exchange vows. As they promise to have and to hold each other from this day forward, they end their promise with these words, "this is my solemn vow." Again, it is the offering word from this week: *selemim*. It is a moment that is marked by their promise, and it is one they will return to and celebrate each year on their anniversary along with many "just because" days, I'm sure!

In our passage today, Hannah makes a solemn vow to God as a promise. If we were to read Hannah's whole story, we would see that her vow is actually a promise wrapped in a gut-wrenching prayer for God to provide her a son. As a woman who was not able to conceive, she was lost in her culture. A barren woman would be missing her identity and her value much like we feel when we've lost a spouse or a career that defined us. As she cries out to the Lord, she tells the priest she is pouring out her soul. Isn't that imagery reminiscent of our reading from yesterday when Mary poured out the oil on Jesus. Hannah held nothing back from God in her request and in return, she held nothing back in the vow she makes.

God, in His faithfulness and compassion, answered her prayer and Hannah's response was to be thankful and keep her vow. She took her son back to the temple and to the priest Eli. Alongside her burnt offering, she surrenders her son in one of the most dramatic offers of thanksgiving contained in the Scripture. Perhaps it is because I am a parent that my heart is in awe of Hannah. The closest I've come to releasing my child into the hands of another person is dropping them off at camp for a couple of weeks or college for a couple of months. Yet Hannah presented her son at the temple where he would "stay there permanently" (1 Sam. 1:22 CEB). It was a lifetime vow.

When Jesus entered this earth, His life was a vow to us, an offering. He chose to give His life for ours and He will never break that vow. In response to His faithfulness and compassion, we have a choice to offer ourselves to Him, a *selemim*.

As a pastor, I know after a bride and groom make their vows and walk down the aisle to cheers and celebration, they will have to choose to keep those vows every day going forward. They will have to cling to those words in the midst of pain and disappointment. They will need to claim those words in seasons of change. Those are the moments when the real value of our vows become evident. We have a choice to offer our vow to the Lord and we have a choice every day to be faithful to that vow.

THE PRAYER

Lord, we recommit ourselves to You. We remember our baptism and we are thankful for the gift of salvation and the relationship You offer. May our vow be as strong today as it was the first day we claimed faith for ourselves. Amen.

THE QUESTIONS

- Have you walked through seasons where you struggled with your commitment as a follower of Jesus? How did you make it through?
- What encouragement do you find knowing that Jesus has made a vow to you that He will never break?

Day 31

Give It Away

PSALM 145:3-7

Great is the Lord and most worthy of praise;
    his greatness no one can fathom.
One generation commends your works to another;
    they tell of your mighty acts.
They speak of the glorious splendor of your majesty—
    and I will meditate on your wonderful works.
They tell of the power of your awesome works—
    and I will proclaim your great deeds.
They celebrate your abundant goodness
    and joyfully sing of your righteousness.

CONSIDER THIS

Have you ever withheld your praise? Don't be too quick to answer, but think about it. Have you ever been frustrated or distracted by one thing that you just didn't feel like offering praise? I've witnessed it in others and—I hate to admit it—I've been guilty of this offense myself.

When we are distracted by busyness or the circumstances of our days, we can forget to give our praise to God. Maybe your day has been full and you just didn't get around to thanking God for the new mercies that met you this morning. Or you forgot to thank God for getting you to work safely or thank Him for even providing you with work today. Take a moment to thank the Lord for something.

In his psalm, David sings his praise to God, but as I read it, he is not alone. There is a generation praising God. As I read this psalm, I envision David with a choir representing a whole generation. They sing of God's glorious splendor and in response, David meditates on His wonderful works. The generational choir sings of God's power and David responds back with God's great deeds. It's this beautiful vision of building off of one another, pointing to God's goodness and anticipating what God will continue to do.

There's a lesson in here for us. Maybe two. First, the power of multigenerational worship is beyond imagination. We need to be combining our voices to not only tell of God's mighty acts, but to be praying together for the Spirit's outpouring. We need to be surrendering our praise as a cross-generational choir.

Second, let's not withhold our praise of the generations behind us. I want to be kind as I write this because I'm aware of my own shortcomings, but we cannot become a "get off my lawn" type of person. Do you know what I mean? Instead of waiting for the generations behind us to reach some invisible "you must be this big to participate" line, let's surrender our praise for where they are and what the Holy Spirit is doing in their lives right now. We might be surprised to find that God is using them to spread the gospel more than us. Our recognition and praise of the generations behind us will build them up and make them stronger.

There is a story the people of the Solomon Islands tell. If they want to cut down a tree that seems too difficult, they yell negative things at it and the tree will die and fall to the ground. This story may seem crazy, but if we exchange people for trees, we can see the truth. Low self-esteem and self-harm are all too common as a result of the negative voices that bombard their hearts. We have an opportunity to call out their best with our gratitude and call out what God is doing. Surrendering our thanks has powerful effects on people.

As we practice giving away our thanksgiving, it does two things: it creates a habit in us and it raises others up. I have a good friend who might be better than anyone I know in this practice. He always says, when you are given a platform, give it away. In other words, when you have a place of position or opportunity, always be willing to step aside and celebrate someone else. Surrender your praise to them. You may not have a platform, but you have praise that can encourage and raise up those around you. Surrendering your praise and commending the work of God in the life of another is commending the Lord Himself.

Let's not be too busy or distracted to pour out our praise to God or others. Let's give it away!

THE PRAYER

Lord, forgive us for when we have been too busy to give You praise. Wake us each morning with a word of praise on our lips and help us pour out our praise on others for Your glory. Amen.

THE QUESTIONS

- Who can you praise and raise up today? How do you think this will affect their day?
- In what ways have you allowed distraction and busyness to keep you from thanking God?

Day 32
Celebration!

LUKE 15:20-24 So he got up and went to his father.

"But while he was still a long way off, his father saw him and was filled with compassion for him; he ran to his son, threw his arms around him and kissed him.

"The son said to him, 'Father, I have sinned against heaven and against you. I am no longer worthy to be called your son.'

"But the father said to his servants, 'Quick! Bring the best robe and put it on him. Put a ring on his finger and sandals on his feet. Bring the fattened calf and kill it. Let's have a feast and celebrate. For this son of mine was dead and is alive again; he was lost and is found.' So they began to celebrate."

CONSIDER THIS

In the early '80s the music group Kool and the Gang released a song called "Celebration." Yes, I'm actually quoting a pop band in our devotional time. Singing the lyrics, we learned that there was a party going on, a celebration, and we were invited to bring our whole selves to it including our good times and laughter because they were going to celebrate with us. In our passage today, there is a party going on and we are supposed to celebrate and invite others to celebrate with us!

I have some good news for you today. Embracing a life of surrender isn't something to be afraid of, but it is something that can bring great joy and peace within community. It's in surrender that we experience the transforming power of God and so can those around us.

When the Israelites brought a peace offering for the Lord, a small portion was burned on the altar, another portion went to the priest, but the largest portion was shared with friends and family. When we develop a habit of giving our thanks to God, it spills out in the way we live in community. Our joys are shared as well as our prayers.

In our passage from Luke, we are reading the end of a story which is actually the end of a trilogy. Jesus has been teaching on the joy of finding what has been lost as a way to illustrate the elation of God when His children repent of their sins and come home to the grace that pursues them. It's one of the most expressive parables in the Gospels. Within this story, we see the son who has walked away from his father and lived a sinful life, but who now asks for forgiveness. What I love in this story is that we don't read that the father first lectures the boy on his life choices or tells him that he will accept him back only if the son promises to never do it again. No, the joy that is felt comes because the father loves so deeply and with great mercy and that is something to celebrate with the entire community.

When we give our thanks to our Father, we should share it with others. Give thanks to God in a celebration of worship. Give thanks to God by opening your home and sharing a meal. Give thanks to God by going out into your community and welcoming those who have not yet found their way home. Surrender your praise by sharing with others. There's a party going on right here and it's a celebration of salvation that comes from the unending grace of our Lord Jesus Christ. It is a celebration that we offer as a surrender of thanks and through which transformation comes not just for ourselves, but those around us.

THE PRAYER

Lord, we celebrate the love You have shown as a Father who runs after His children and we pray that we show the same outpouring of mercy to those around us who need to be loved. Let us be aware of those who also don't feel included and may we be the ones that welcome them home in Your name. Amen.

THE QUESTIONS

- When was the last time you celebrated the grace of God in your life?
- Who can you invite into a relationship with Christ so they can experience His compassion and mercy?

Part Five

Surrender Past for Freedom (Sin Offering)

Day 33
Oops!

LEVITICUS 4:1-3 The LORD said to Moses, "Say to the Israelites: 'When anyone sins unintentionally and does what is forbidden in any of the LORD's commands—

"'If the anointed priest sins, bringing guilt on the people, he must bring to the LORD a young bull without defect as a sin offering for the sin he has committed.'"

CONSIDER THIS

How many of us have uttered the word *oops* when we've done something we didn't mean to do? The history of this exclamation can be traced back to the seventeenth and eighteenth centuries where it used to mean "lift up from a day of sorrow or regret." The mistakes of our past often drag us down and we need a lift.

This week, our offering passage in Leviticus teaches us about the sin offering. I know it seems like all offerings address sin, but this particular offering was used to seek atonement for a specific category of sins and we'll see how God uses the fourth type of offering to meet us in the mistakes of the burdens from our past that we carry into the present. This week we will see how the lessons from the sin offering help us respond and find freedom from our brokenness and regret, our thoughts, excuses, and shame.

The sin offering, or the *chattath*, was sometimes referred to as the purification offering and was different from the other offerings we've read about. First, *chattath* focused more on the sin than the sacrifice. Second, contrary to what you might assume given its name, this particular offering was given to seek purification for inadvertent sins and not deliberate ones. It was also given for sins where restitution was not possible. What does that mean? Think back to the very beginning of this Lenten season when we reflected on the fact that the world is not as it was designed. "On earth as it is in heaven" is what we long for because our fallen nature has spoiled God's original creation and by ourselves, we cannot experience the presence of a Holy God.

Sin isn't just a label we put on choices we make, but it is the condition we find ourselves in because of the original sin in the garden. In short, we are sinners in need of a Savior and it is only through the provision of atonement we find forgiveness. Before Jesus came to earth, God provided a temporary atonement for the sins of the people and there was a division of inadvertent sins and deliberate sins. The sin offering was the way to receive purification for inadvertent sins like, *Oops! I worked on the Sabbath*. Or *Oops! I forgot to participate in a cleansing ritual*. It also provided purification at festivals or when a woman had become unclean due to childbirth.

The most important element in the sacrifice was the blood, but for us to understand, we need to reverse the way we look at blood. For us, when we see blood we think of something that is unclean, but for the Israelites, blood was like bleach. It was only through the blood that they could be made clean. What could wash away my sin and what can make me whole again? Anyone humming the great old hymn, "Nothing but the Blood" right now? This week, let's continue to prepare our hearts and create intentional space to encounter God as we surrender the sins of the past for the freedom He promises.

THE PRAYER

Lord, thank You for making a way for us to have the gift of Your presence even though we don't deserve it. We are stained with our sins, but You have made us clean again. Amen.

THE QUESTIONS

- When you realize that you have made a mistake and sinned inadvertently, how does that change the way you pray for forgiveness?
- What are some sins you have committed that you have not brought to God and confessed?

Day 34
Pinned!

GENESIS 32:22-30 That night Jacob got up and took his two wives, his two female servants and his eleven sons and crossed the ford of the Jabbok. After he had sent them across the stream, he sent over all his possessions. So Jacob was left alone, and a man wrestled with him till daybreak. When the man saw that he could not overpower him, he touched the socket of Jacob's hip so that his hip was wrenched as he wrestled with the man. Then the man said, "Let me go, for it is daybreak."

But Jacob replied, "I will not let you go unless you bless me."

The man asked him, "What is your name?"

"Jacob," he answered.

Then the man said, "Your name will no longer be Jacob, but Israel, because you have struggled with God and with humans and have overcome."

Jacob said, "Please tell me your name."

But he replied, "Why do you ask my name?" Then he blessed him there.

> So Jacob called the place Peniel, saying, "It is because I saw God face to face, and yet my life was spared."

GENESIS 33:19-20 For a hundred pieces of silver, he bought from the sons of Hamor, the father of Shechem, the plot of ground where he pitched his tent. There he set up an altar and called it El Elohe Israel.

CONSIDER THIS

I'm a fan of many different sports, but wrestling is not one of them. I don't really understand it as a sport and it feels one-dimensional in terms of how to win (if you're a fan of wrestling, I apologize), but there is one professional wrestling term that we should all learn. It's the term *submission*. When one wrestler chooses to yield to the other, he must submit.

In our altar story today, Jacob experiences a shift in his life because he surrenders, or, in wrestling terms, through submission. You may recall that Jacob is the son of Isaac and grandson of Abraham. As a young man he cheated his brother, Esau, out of his rightful inheritance, which created deep conflict between them. In order to save his life, Jacob ran away and after a period of time, married Leah and Rachel. Just prior to our passage today, Jacob found out that his brother, Esau, was on his way to see him and after many years of being estranged from him, Jacob was afraid to face the sins of his past.

The night before he would have to face his brother, Jacob wrestled with a man who we find out is an angel of the Lord. By this time, Jacob is ninety-seven years old so I cannot imagine he was much of a match for the angel, but they wrestled through the night. It might seem that Jacob is winning because the angel calls time-out, but it is actually Jacob who realized this was a pinnacle moment for him. He had a choice. He was at a proverbial fork in the road. Would he continue down the path of denying his sin and running away from the consequences or would he open himself up to find freedom by surrendering to the Lord?

Jacob, in asking for a blessing, demonstrates his willingness to submit to God and repent of his past. The wrestling match became a physical representation of Jacob's heart. God had the power to force Jacob, but He didn't want to pin Jacob down to win. God wanted him to willingly submit. It is when we choose to surrender that we experience the shift in our lives of transformation. And when Jacob surrendered, God changed his name to Israel as a declaration of his transformed heart. Jacob faced the sins of his past and God provided freedom of a new future.

Are you wrestling with God in any area of your life? Is there a place where you are holding on to the sins of the past or running away from the consequences? We have an invitation to yield, to offer submission to God, and allow God to transform us.

THE PRAYER

Lord, how long will we run away from our sin? We want a new life and a new name that reflects how You have changed our hearts. We surrender all to You! Amen.

THE QUESTIONS

- When have you felt like you were wrestling with God? Was there something you were holding on to that you needed to let go of and give to God?
- Where would you like to see God do a transforming work in your life?

Day 35
Cracked Pots

GALATIANS 2:19-21 "For through the law I died to the law so that I might live for God. I have been crucified with Christ and I no longer live, but Christ lives in me. The life I now live in the body, I live by faith in the Son of God, who loved me and gave himself for me. I do not set aside the grace of God, for if righteousness could be gained through the law, Christ died for nothing!"

CONSIDER THIS

How many of you have heard the story of the boy who carried water in two clay pots hanging on either end of a long pole? Each day he filled up the pots and carried them down the path to his master's house. One pot was perfect, but the other pot was broken with several cracks, so water leaked out and it was never able to deliver the full amount of water. At the end of the year the broken pot felt defeated and apologized to the boy about its imperfections. Yet the boy would not accept the apologies. He told the broken pot that he knew all about his brokenness, so he scattered seed on that side of the path. Because the water leaked out, the seeds were watered and bloomed to be a blessing to others. The boy saw that new life could come from imperfect places. Praise the Lord!

If we were to measure our lives against the law as the Israelites did, we would find ourselves much like the pot who was defeated when he looked at his imperfections. As grateful as I am that God made a temporary way for atonement before Jesus, I am more grateful that it is through Christ's death that my imperfections are made perfect. Paul, in his letter to the Galatians, is clear that measured against the law, his life would be lost. In fact, it is the law which condemned him and Christ who freed him.

The Israelites knew that freedom from their brokenness could only come from the blood of the sacrifices which were surrendered at the altar. "For the life of a creature is in the blood, and I have given it to you to make atonement for yourselves on the altar; it is the blood that makes atonement for one's life" (Lev. 17:11). Slow down and read that again and make it personal. It is Jesus's blood that makes atonement for my life. Jesus is the lifeblood and only through Him can we have life.

Paul reminds the Galatians that they don't have to try and patch up their broken places by using the law. Jesus takes all of our brokenness and uses it for His glory to create a new witness of His transforming power. Have you felt imperfect during this Lenten journey? Discovered any new broken places? The good news that Paul shared with the Galatians is true for us today. Our brokenness is made whole through the sacrifice from Jesus so we can surrender those imperfections to Jesus. This week as you are reflecting on the parts of your life that are imperfect, remember that we live by faith and are loved by the Father.

THE PRAYER

Jesus, thank You for paying our debts so we are not shackled by our sins. Give us an opportunity today to encourage someone who feels broken and remind them that through You, they can be used for Your glory. Amen.

THE QUESTIONS

- What does it mean to you that you no longer live, but Christ lives in you?
- How have you tried to pay the debt of your sin by yourself?

Day 36
Reverse Course

LUKE 22:31-34 "Simon, Simon, Satan has asked to sift all of you as wheat. But I have prayed for you, Simon, that your faith may not fail. And when you have turned back, strengthen your brothers."

But he replied, "Lord, I am ready to go with you to prison and to death."

Jesus answered, "I tell you, Peter, before the rooster crows today, you will deny three times that you know me."

CONSIDER THIS

Have you ever watched an action movie when the main character is in a car chase and then he finds himself head-to-head with the enemy? Racing toward each other at full throttle you know that someone is going to have to throw their car into reverse and turn back and it's almost always the good guy that's willing to reverse course. That's the image in my mind as I read one of my favorite verses. Simon, also known as Peter, was a dedicated disciple, throwing himself into every situation and every conversation whether he should have or not. At the end of the Passover meal an argument breaks out among the disciples over who is the greatest. Jesus breaks up the argument by telling them that in the kingdom of God, there is a reversal, and the least will be the greatest. Then without missing a beat, Jesus looks at Simon and tells him that the enemy is about to tempt him—to sift him as wheat. In other words, he's about to go head-to-head with the enemy.

Here, in one of my favorite verses, Jesus tells Simon that He has already prayed for him and His prayer is that Simon won't fail. Let that sink in for a moment. The enemy is a prowling lion who comes after Jesus's followers, but Jesus intercedes through prayer. This does not mean that tempting doesn't come and it doesn't mean that Simon will overcome the temptation. In fact, he doesn't. Peter fails. But that is not the end of his story. Again, without missing a beat, Jesus says "And when you have turned back," or another way to read this is, "When you have reversed course, I have a plan for you." Jesus knows Peter will fail, but He also knows Peter will use his experience to help others.

Have you ever made a mess of your life? Did you experience regret? Like our altar story, we can surrender our regret and let Jesus use it for His glory and His purpose. Regret doesn't have to be altogether bad. When the Holy Spirit uses regret as a motivation to reverse our course, then Jesus will give us freedom. But when we wallow in regret and we beat ourselves up over our mistakes, our sins become our shackles.

Peter reverses course because Jesus does not abandon him, and Jesus does not abandon us. In fact, He is interceding for us with His prayers. And when we surrender regret to the Lord, we experience the freedom of second chances. I love that Jesus uses the word, "when" and not "if." He tells Peter, in effect, "When you turn back, you will be equipped to use your experience to help others." The sin of our past regret is not our future. Through the grace of Jesus, Peter finds redemption just like we do. As Paul wrote to the Philippians about his own struggles, "Forgetting what is behind and straining toward what is ahead, I press on toward the goal to win the prize for which God has called me heavenward in Christ Jesus" (3:13–14).

Today, in the intentional space you have created for the Lord, reflect on where you are headed. Do you need to reverse course in any area of your life? Are you holding on to any mistakes? Surrender your regret and head in the direction of Jesus's love, knowing that the surrender of regret can be used as a witness to God's grace.

THE PRAYER

Lord, Your grace is enough. Grant us the ability to recognize when we are face to face with the enemy and have the wisdom to turn away. We give You everything we have and pray that the Holy Spirit will use it as a witness to Your goodness. Amen.

THE QUESTIONS

- What regret are you holding on to that you need to surrender?
- Where can you use your life experience to encourage and strengthen someone else?

Day 37
Mind over Matter

PHILIPPIANS 4:8-9 Finally, brothers and sisters, whatever is true, whatever is noble, whatever is right, whatever is pure, whatever is lovely, whatever is admirable—if anything is excellent or praiseworthy—think about such things. Whatever you have learned or received or heard from me or seen in me—put it into practice. And the God of peace will be with you.

CONSIDER THIS

The mind is a powerful tool. We know that where the mind leads, our bodies and actions will follow. When we dwell on areas of temptation and we hold on to ideas which direct us in ways which are not holy, our entire lives can be dismantled because sin has already taken root. Yesterday we saw how the enemy will use regret to get us off course, and today we see that he can use the thoughts in our minds to do the same.

In Paul's letter to the Philippians, he addresses a problem we all have, controlling our minds. Like an unattended toddler, our minds can get into trouble within seconds. We get distracted. We see something exciting. We get bored with what we have and—*poof*—our mind has latched on to something it shouldn't have. The best way to steer a child away from what will harm them is to put something better in front of them. Remove the heirloom crystal bowl and replace it with a sturdy interactive book. Turn off the television show full of violence and replace it with education or music.

The Philippian church was one of the first churches Paul started in Eastern Europe and they were facing opposition. Paul wanted to remind them that their lives were to be an expression of Jesus and so they needed to keep their minds focused on Christ. If they could guard their minds, their actions would follow—they needed to cling to thoughts which were true, noble, right, pure, lovely, admirable, excellent, or praiseworthy. This would be a common encouragement of Paul. He told other believers to "set your minds on things above" (Col. 3:2), "take captive every thought to make it obedient to Christ" (2 Cor. 10:5), and "be transformed by the renewing of your mind" (Rom. 12:2).

Jesus also knew the power of our thoughts to lead us either toward Him or away from Him. When Jesus healed the paralytic who was lowered through a roof by his friends, the Pharisees and the teachers of the law began to question in their minds how Jesus could forgive sins. Though they did not address Jesus directly, He knew their thoughts and chastised them saying, "Why are you thinking these things in your hearts?" (Luke 5:22).

Jesus is everything Paul listed for the Philippians beginning with the truth. If we are to be altar'd by the Holy Spirit, we must surrender our thoughts and grasp hold of the truth of Jesus. When you begin to feel your mind wander, pull your focus back to Paul's encouragement and ask yourself if your mind is over all other matter.

THE PRAYER

Lord, our minds so often wander. We are tempted by what we see and what we hear, but we also know that You are the way, the truth, and the life. Guide our minds back to You so that what we do is a reflection on where we have focused our minds. Amen.

THE QUESTIONS

- What thoughts are crowding out the truth of God's words?
- In what ways have your thoughts kept you from being fully committed to Jesus and what can you do this week to replace those thoughts with what is true, noble, right, pure, lovely, admirable, excellent, or praiseworthy?

Day 38

Excuses, Excuses

2 CORINTHIANS 7:9-11 Yet now I am happy, not because you were made sorry, but because your sorrow led you to repentance. For you became sorrowful as God intended and so were not harmed in any way by us. Godly sorrow brings repentance that leads to salvation and leaves no regret, but worldly sorrow brings death. See what this godly sorrow has produced in you: what earnestness, what eagerness to clear yourselves, what indignation, what alarm, what longing, what concern, what readiness to see justice done. At every point you have proved yourselves to be innocent in this matter.

CONSIDER THIS

In the altar story this week, Jacob ran away from his sin for years. He allowed the mistakes of his youth to keep him from maintaining a relationship with his brother. It wasn't until he wrestled with God and surrendered his life that Jacob was transformed and given a new name. Looking back at his story,

I wonder how many times, before his wrestling match, he had replayed that scene in his head of cheating his brother out of his inheritance? Had he tried to reframe his actions in a way that allowed him to justify his actions? Had he made excuses for his behavior?

When we become aware of our sin, we will often make excuses to avoid taking responsibility. We justify our behavior and we blame the other person. The danger in making excuses is we speak our own words over a situation instead of listening to the voice of the Lord. Making excuses is what Paul calls worldly sorrow and it just makes us feel sorry for ourselves.

Paul had written several letters to the Corinthian church to correct their behavior. They were known to be disobedient and make excuses rather than take responsibility. In this letter, Paul acknowledges their hurt, but he says that he doesn't regret the redirection. Why? Because Paul says it has caused them to seek repentance. There is a difference between worldly sorrow and godly sorrow. The hurt of the world is meant to beat us down and tell us we have done something bad. The hurt of the Holy Spirit is meant to move to confession where we find redemption.

Paul doesn't want the believers to make excuses for their behavior or to run away from the consequences. He wants them to surrender their excuses to take the responsibility of repentance because Paul knows that they will receive forgiveness. "If we confess our sins, he is faithful and just and will forgive us our sins and purify us from all unrighteousness" (1 John 1:9). Our Lenten journey invites us to open ourselves to godly sorrow and ask the Holy Spirit to show us where we have been justifying our choices. Freedom comes through the forgiveness of Christ and it also frees us to be fully devoted followers of Jesus.

THE PRAYER

Jesus, thank You for leading us to repentance because we might not have gotten there on our own. We know that it is because You love us that it hurts You to see us make excuses for our behavior. We lay it down before You today and ask for You to redeem us. Amen.

THE QUESTIONS

- What excuses have you made for sins in your life? Are you willing to bring them to the Lord and receive forgiveness?
- How does taking responsibility reflect the nature of Christ in our lives?

Day 39
For Shame

ROMANS 8:1-4 Therefore, there is now no condemnation for those who are in Christ Jesus, because through Christ Jesus the law of the Spirit who gives life has set you free from the law of sin and death. For what the law was powerless to do because it was weakened by the flesh, God did by sending his own Son in the likeness of sinful flesh to be a sin offering. And so he condemned sin in the flesh, in order that the righteous requirement of the law might be fully met in us, who do not live according to the flesh but according to the Spirit.

CONSIDER THIS

The enemy loves to shame us because it becomes the voice in our head that tells us we are bad people who do not deserve to be loved, forgiven, or accepted. Yesterday we read a passage from Paul about the correction he gave to the believers in Corinth. Correction is different than shame. Paul has never used the sin and the mistakes of the believers as a way to shame them and tell them they had gone too far to receive forgiveness. Jesus also never used His correction to make someone believe they were not worthy of receiving forgiveness or eternal life. But the enemy will. Satan understands that if he can make us question our identity as children of God that we will hide ourselves away from the loving arms of our Father. This makes shame a dangerous emotion.

In today's culture, we seem to have a love-hate relationship with shame. On the one hand, people will completely disregard any sense of wrongdoing and will stick their heads in the sand believing they can do anything that feels right to them. On the other hand, people will cling to shame and convince themselves they are unlovable. In studying the effects of shame, mental health experts have found that as shame is held in the body, it can lead to issues of self-esteem, isolation, and feelings of humiliation. These are feelings the enemy takes advantage of to keep us enslaved to him, but this has never been the Lord's intent for our lives. In our passage today, Paul tells us that there is no condemnation for followers of Jesus, not because they can do anything they want, but because Jesus's sacrifice has freed us from the shame of sin. When we hold on to shame, we reject the freedom Jesus provides. In verse 3, we read that Jesus laid his life on the altar by dying on the cross as the sin offering for us. Remember that the sin offering was given to seek atonement for our fallen nature, the original sin that we have because of the fall in Genesis 3.

But Jesus gives us freedom from our shame because He says, "As the Father has loved me, so have I loved you. Now remain in my love" (John 15:9). Our shame will make us question who we are because we know our flaws, our thoughts, the excuses we've given, and we know our brokenness. When we surrender our shame, we choose not to live by the lies of the enemy. Surrendering our shame allows us to feel the freedom of grace we have been given. John, the disciple of Jesus, wrote "And now, dear children, continue in him, so that when he appears we may be confident and unashamed before him at his coming" (1 John 2:28).

THE PRAYER

Father, because of Your love we can reject the shame of the enemy. We stand today as beloved children of the Most High King. Thank You for being the sin offering which frees us from condemnation. Amen.

THE QUESTIONS

- How have you felt condemned in your life? Is that condemnation coming from someone else or within you? How does this verse help you feel released?
- How will you live differently today knowing that you are called to live by the Spirit and not the flesh?

Part Six

Surrender Pain for Restoration (Guilt Offering)

Day 40
Pay Up

LEVITICUS 6:1-5 The Lord said to Moses: "If anyone sins and is unfaithful to the Lord by deceiving a neighbor about something entrusted to them or left in their care or about something stolen, or if they cheat their neighbor, or if they find lost property and lie about it, or if they swear falsely about any such sin that people may commit—when they sin in any of these ways and realize their guilt, they must return what they have stolen or taken by extortion, or what was entrusted to them, or the lost property they found, or whatever it was they swore falsely about. They must make restitution in full, add a fifth of the value to it and give it all to the owner on the day they present their guilt offering."

CONSIDER THIS

We are entering the final week of the Lenten season usually referred to as Holy Week. From the Palm Sunday processional to the final Passover meal to the crucifixion and the resurrection, we will see evidence of Jesus's sacrifice not only physically, but emotionally and spiritually. This is also the last of the five offerings from Leviticus. The guilt offering, or the *asam*, was sometimes referred to as the reparation offering and was given to atone for sins, but in contrast to the sin offering from last week, these were sins where restitution could and should be made. In other words, these are the sins that demand payment.

Restitution, or payment for our sins, is required because we are accountable for our obedience to God, the way we treat what is holy and the way we treat others. Notice the connection in this passage of an offense against a neighbor and our faithfulness to the Lord? That is because when we sin, we might be able to repair or replace something that is physically damaged, but there is also relational damage, and that damage can only be fully restored through the grace of God. Over the next few days, we are going to sit with some hard passages and Jesus is going to invite us into doing the hard work of visiting the pain we caused or the pain we've experienced because of others. The great news is that Jesus also promises restoration when we are willing to surrender our pain to Him.

My hope is that you have been taking advantage of the invitation during this Lenten journey to understand the sacrificial system of offerings which God created for the Israelites and see how they anticipate Jesus as the ultimate sacrifice and fulfillment of God's covenant. He was, in fact, a perfect burnt offering, grain offering, peace offering, sin offering, and guilt offering, and because God so loved the world that He gave His only Son as an atonement for sin, we no longer live under these laws. But let's not jump to the end too quickly, because this offering reminds us that we have a debt to be paid. It reminds us that we injure our relationship with God when we are disobedient, and we injure our relationship with others when we sin against them. This week, our offering and altar story helps us learn how to surrender our pain and gain restoration, so that we might respond to disappointment, grudges, and all manner of hurts in a restorative way.

THE PRAYER

Lord Jesus, steady our hearts and give us the courage to surrender our pain to You. Help us also to feel the absolute joy of knowing that You are the sacrifice that was given for our restoration. Amen.

THE QUESTIONS

- Why do you think it was important to connect sin against another person and sin against God? How does that affect how you view sin?
- When you have tried to make restitution for a sin you had committed against another person, did you try to make up for it by doing more or giving back more than you took? Why or why not?

Day 41
Cost of Discipleship

1 CHRONICLES 21:22-24 David said to him, "Let me have the site of your threshing floor so I can build an altar to the LORD, that the plague on the people may be stopped. Sell it to me at the full price."

Araunah said to David, "Take it! Let my lord the king do whatever pleases him. Look, I will give the oxen for the burnt offerings, the threshing sledges for the wood, and the wheat for the grain offering. I will give all this."

But King David replied to Araunah, "No, I insist on paying the full price. I will not take for the LORD what is yours or sacrifice a burnt offering that costs me nothing."

CONSIDER THIS

In the corporate world, the phrase "the cost of doing business" is self-explanatory. There is an expected cost associated with leading or owning a business. It may be purchasing a building, paying employees, or buying a new vehicle, but I don't know many people who jump into a life of discipleship and ask about the cost.

In our altar story this week, we read that "Satan rose up against Israel and incited David to take a census of Israel" (1 Chron. 21:1) instead of trusting in God's promise to keep Israel secure. As a result, a plague swept through his people and seventy thousand of them died. David knew he had sinned against God and must make restitution. I admit that as I read the many stories of altars built by David and sacrifices offered to God, it was this story that grabbed my heart because when David was offered an easy way out, he refused to take it.

The owner of the threshing floor where David planned to create an altar space was willing to give it to him for free. How many of us would turn down a generous offer like that? The path of least resistance and the pain of least pain. And yet David knew that living a life honoring to Lord meant taking responsibility for his sin and that asks something of us.

He is right. Living as if following Christ has no cost is like charging a credit card to its limit and then asking the bank to change the balance back to zero. Just as Paul wrote, "What shall we say, then? Shall we go on sinning so that grace may increase? By no means! We are those who have died to sin; how can we live in it any longer?" (Rom. 6:1–2). Don't get me wrong, discipleship is not a works-based system, but it does require our obedience and devotion.

Christians are fond of celebrating the lavish grace and unfailing compassion of Jesus, but we are sometimes hesitant to discuss the expectations of following Christ. But what a disservice to the Lord, especially this week as we remember that pain that He willingly endured so we could receive that grace. Theologian Dietrich Bonhoeffer reminds us that "salvation is free, but discipleship will cost you your life." What is discipleship costing you right now?

THE PRAYER

Jesus, thank You for paying the cost of our sin. Search our hearts today and know our anxious thoughts. Stir within us the willingness to be a disciple willing to pay anything in order to share Your grace with others and to be a reflection of Your love. Amen.

THE QUESTIONS

- Have you ever experienced a time where being a disciple cost you something important in your life?
- What are you willing to give to follow Jesus?

Day 42

Does Not Meet Expectations

2 TIMOTHY 4:16-18 At my first defense, no one came to my support, but everyone deserted me. May it not be held against them. But the Lord stood at my side and gave me strength, so that through me the message might be fully proclaimed, and all the Gentiles might hear it. And I was delivered from the lion's mouth. The Lord will rescue me from every evil attack and will bring me safely to his heavenly kingdom. To him be glory for ever and ever. Amen.

CONSIDER THIS

As a student, I would dread the possibility that my report card might have the box checked for "Does Not Meet Expectations." I never wanted to disappoint a teacher or a friend, and yet there have been many times I'm sure I have, just as I have been disappointed by them. As we are learning, sin has a heavy influence on our relationships with one another. Being altar'd is going to require us to surrender our disappointment; to be willing to let go of the expectations others have not met in our lives and the pain it has caused.

In Paul's final letter to his apprentice, friend, and co-laborer Timothy, he is truthful in sharing his disappointment. After years and years of serving God faithfully, of teaching and encouraging other disciples, Paul has found himself in prison once again. However, by now he has developed a reputation based on his teachings of Jesus and being associated with Paul was dangerous. Paul tells Timothy that even though he has sacrificed for others and been faithful to other believers, everyone has deserted him. Can you empathize? Have you ever felt the pain of being deserted by people you thought were your friends? Being disappointed by someone may seem small compared to tragic offenses we have experienced by others, but even the small pains in relationship can intensify when we don't release them.

Being part of the body of Christ does not mean that you won't experience disappointment, hurt, and bitterness when someone fails to meet expectations, but we can choose to surrender that pain to God. Truthfully, it might even be harder to let go of the pain we feel when it happens within the community of believers because we have higher expectations of them. Think of the passage we read several weeks ago of Jesus praying in the garden of Gethsemane. He asked His closest disciples to stay with Him while He prayed, and

He expected them to offer support during His dark night of the soul.

> Then Jesus went with his disciples to a place called Gethsemane, and he said to them, "Sit here while I go over there and pray." He took Peter and the two sons of Zebedee along with him, and he began to be sorrowful and troubled. Then he said to them, "My soul is overwhelmed with sorrow to the point of death. Stay here and keep watch with me." . . .
>
> Then he returned to his disciples and found them sleeping. "Couldn't you men keep watch with me for one hour?" he asked Peter. (Matt. 26:36–38, 40)

The disciples failed to meet the expectations of Jesus three times. If I were Jesus, I'd be ready to throw in the towel of our relationship. And yet we learn from both Jesus and Paul that the reaction we are invited to have to the pain of disappointment is surrender, releasing it to God. What did Paul say? "May it not be held against them." Paul did not wallow in his disappointment, holding on to the pain, but he turned his eyes to the Lord for strength and comfort.

Walking in Jesus's footsteps this Holy Week, we will see Him face disappointment over and over again, but Jesus did not allow disappointment to distract Him from fulfilling the life mission that would give us salvation. As you face disappointments, are you willing to surrender it to the Lord so He can strengthen you?

THE PRAYER

Lord, disappointment seems like such a small pain and yet when we hold it, the pain grows. Would You begin to heal the small wounds that we carry so they do not become larger ones? Thank You for helping us release our disappointment so that we do not carry it. Amen.

THE QUESTIONS

- Where are you holding on to disappointment in others? Can you release that today and trust Jesus with that pain?
- Learning from Paul's experience, what are some of the positive consequences of releasing the pain of disappointment?

Day 43
Grudge Match

MATTHEW 5:23-24 "Therefore, if you are offering your gift at the altar and there remember that your brother or sister has something against you, leave your gift there in front of the altar. First go and be reconciled to them; then come and offer your gift."

CONSIDER THIS

I'm a huge college football fan. My friends and family look forward to the start of a new football season months before it begins and we talk about the highlights and the near misses months afterward. I've also noticed an interesting phenomenon that happens close to a new season. Battle lines begin to be drawn. When late summer arrives, the team jerseys come out and the big talk of past beatdowns get thrown around like challenge flags. I've seen the same behavior in people who hold grudges for past hurts and emotional injuries. When we hold grudges, we draw battle lines, and we unearth buried pain just to put it on and carry it around like team jerseys.

Yesterday we focused on not withholding forgiveness, but actually paying forward the forgiveness as a response to our relationship with Christ. Today, we go a step further. In our passage, Jesus is preaching His Sermon on the Mount. In this teaching, He points back to the human behavior addressed by the law in the Old Testament and He gives it new meaning. Jesus recounts, "You have heard it said you shall not murder, but I say that anyone who is angry with a brother or sister will face the same judgment" (Matt. 5:21–22, author's paraphrase). In a twist on previous commands, Jesus tells us to reconcile with the person before we bring our offering to God.

Our relationship with others affects our relationship with our Lord. It is the evidence of our heart and our holiness. How can we pursue holiness if we are holding a grudge? As the famous saying goes, holding a grudge is like drinking poison and expecting the other person to die. Surrendering forgiveness may mean you have to let go first and let the response of the other person remain with God.

In his letter to the Ephesians, Paul tells the believers to pursue restoration immediately because the longer we hold our anger, the more space we give the enemy to do his work. "'In your anger do not sin': Do not let the sun go down while you are still angry, and do not give the devil a foothold" (Eph. 4:26–27). It begs the question, for whom are we making space? During Lent we've focused on building an altar with our lives to create space to encounter God, but Jesus teaches that holding on to the pain another has caused us creates space for the enemy to work.

The enemy loves to destroy relationships, especially within the body of Christ because it can tear at the fabric of our community and our effectiveness to reach others with the good news of Jesus. It takes one person to forgive, but it takes two to reconcile and in reconciliation, Jesus exchanges peace for pain. "For he himself is our peace, who has made the two groups one and has destroyed the barrier, the dividing wall of hostility, by setting aside in his flesh the law with its commands and regulations. His purpose was to create in himself one new humanity out of the two, thus making peace" (Eph. 2:14–15). So, it's time to take off the jersey and lay down the grudge so through the Holy Spirit, we are made one in Christ.

THE PRAYER

Lord, show us if any of our brothers or sisters have something against us. Lead us to take the first step toward reconciliation so that we may worship You with a full and free heart. Amen.

THE QUESTIONS

- Why is it your responsibility to seek reconciliation first and not wait for the other person?
- Who do you need to reconcile with before bringing your offering to God?

Day 44

Sticks and Stones

1 JOHN 4:19-21 We love because he first loved us. Whoever claims to love God yet hates a brother or sister is a liar. For whoever does not love their brother and sister, whom they have seen, cannot love God, whom they have not seen. And he has given us this command: Anyone who loves God must also love their brother and sister.

CONSIDER THIS

The pain of sin comes in many different forms, but possibly the most painful and the most prevalent is the pain that comes from our words. As a child you probably heard that sticks and stones may break your bones, but words will never hurt you, but that is a lie. Our words have a lasting effect on others. They remain firmly planted in our memories and can rear their ugly heads at any moment. And for some reason, the power of negative words seems to be so much stronger than the power of positive ones.

It is Thursday of Holy Week and many of us will attend church services tonight, remembering the last supper Jesus had with His disciples and how Jesus washed their feet as a sign of servanthood. Yet it was on this night that two of His disciples would hurt Jesus with their words. Judas's betrayal was premeditated. He had gone to the chief priests and officers of the temple guard to plot how he might betray Jesus. Peter's denial was predicted. Even as he promised his loyalty, Jesus knew that Peter would falter.

At the Passover meal, Jesus turned to the disciples and told them, "Love one another. As I have loved you, so you must love one another. By this everyone will know that you are my disciples, if you love one another" (John 13:34–35). Surrendering the pain of betrayal and denial might just take the strength of Jesus, but it is in following after His example that we can find restoration.

It is not enough to just love the Savior who gave His life for you. The evidence of your love must be in how you love others. Remember that being altar'd creates space to encounter Jesus, offers a surrender, and experiences a shift or transformation in our lives. Loving others is the evidence of a shift in our hearts and in our behavior. As you enter into the worship space to remember Jesus's last meal with His disciples, let it be a time of laying down the pain of words that have been spoken about you or over you. Lay down the words that you have said to others confessing that they did not show love to your brother or sister. As you surrender, allow the Lord to replace that pain with His mercy and restore the wounded places of your heart.

THE PRAYER

Jesus, we are sorry for the ways we have betrayed You and denied You. We are sorry we have not loved You with our whole hearts and we have not loved our neighbors. Forgive us we pray. Amen.

THE QUESTIONS

- What wounds have you carried from words that have been spoken to you or about you that you can lay down today?
- What wounds have you caused by your words? Are you able to confess and ask for forgiveness?

Day 45
Credit Rating

MATTHEW 6:14-15 "For if you forgive other people when they sin against you, your heavenly Father will also forgive you. But if you do not forgive others their sins, your Father will not forgive your sins."

CONSIDER THIS

In the North American culture, debt is a common state of life. We accumulate debt when we buy a house, finance a car, or take out a credit card. Being a debtor is even encouraged as a way to establish a credit rating, but in the world of God's kingdom, being a debtor doesn't require us to pay it back, but to pay it forward. On Good Friday we see Jesus wipe away our sins' eternal consequences and through His grace we experience restoration.

In the early days of His ministry, Jesus taught about prayer in His famous Sermon on the Mount. This is where we learn the Lord's Prayer that many of us recite every week. In the prayer, we ask the Lord to forgive us as we forgive those who have hurt us. Jesus knows that our sin creates a debt that we cannot repay so He has chosen to become the payment for our sin. In response to the payment we've received, we are expected to pay it forward by forgiving others. Our surrender of forgiveness becomes the proof of our salvation.

It may seem odd to connect forgiveness with pain. Shouldn't it feel good to forgive? Maybe it should, but it often feels like a sacrifice. We numb the pain of an emotional or physical injury by withholding our forgiveness instead of offering it to God. Jesus tells us to flip the script. Don't hold back but be willing to pay extra.

We know the disciples struggled with forgiveness like many of us do. In the Gospel of Luke, Jesus tells them that their forgiveness credit should have no limits. "'So watch yourselves. If your brother or sister sins against you, rebuke them; and if they repent, forgive them. Even if they sin against you seven times in a day and seven times come back to you saying "I repent" you must forgive them.' The apostles said to the Lord, 'Increase our faith!'" (Luke 17:3–5). I'm pretty sure my response would have been the same as the disciples— increase my faith because I cannot forgive that many times out of my own strength.

The Greek word for forgiveness in our Matthew passage (*aphiemi*) means to let go or send away. Don't let the pain of someone else's sin settle on you as a burden you have to carry but send it away to the Lord who teaches us that there is no limit to forgiveness. Let's consider it a privilege to pay forgiveness forward. There is a saying that "hurt people, hurt people," so let us be an example that forgiven people, forgive people.

Envision the shape of the cross. It has two beams, one vertical and the other horizontal. If there is just the vertical beam, it's not a cross, it's a post. And if there is just the horizontal beam, it just lies on the ground. The cross asks us to attend to both the vertical relationship we have with the triune God and the relationship we have with others.

There is no greater example of love than what we see on Good Friday. After being arrested, Jesus is brutally beaten. He's given an opportunity to fight for His life, but instead He chooses to follow God's plan for salvation by becoming the sacrificial lamb that takes on the sin of the world so the world can receive restoration. May we follow the example of Christ with the words He spoke on the cross, "Father, forgive them" (Luke 23:34).

THE PRAYER

Merciful God, thank You for the forgiveness that You have lavished on us over and over again. When we feel tempted to withhold our forgiveness, remind us that we can pay it forward through the power of the Holy Spirit. Amen.

THE QUESTIONS

- When have you experienced Jesus's forgiveness in your own life?
- What emotions have you felt when you have forgiven someone? Was it painful? Was it freeing?

Day 46

Account Access

JAMES 5:15-16, 19-20 And the prayer offered in faith will make the sick person well; the Lord will raise them up. If they have sinned, they will be forgiven. Therefore confess your sins to each other and pray for each other so that you may be healed. The prayer of a righteous person is powerful and effective. . . . My brothers and sisters, if one of you should wander from the truth and someone should bring that person back, remember this: Whoever turns a sinner from the error of their way will save them from death and cover over a multitude of sins.

CONSIDER THIS

Cybersecurity is a real concern. Many of our banks, large corporations, and even personal accounts are vulnerable to financial attacks and identity theft so new measures of authentication and protection are constantly being developed. And once again, the world of God's kingdom is upside down when compared to today's culture. While the world is putting up firewalls and protective measures, the Lord is telling us to tear walls down and give access to our lives through accountability partners because it is only in opening ourselves up to Jesus and to other believers that we will experience the transforming power of the Holy Spirit.

We have walked faithfully through this Lenten season, learning about the Old Testament's sacrificial system, studying altar stories where people have encountered God, and we have been challenged to embrace a life of surrender. The day after the disciples witnessed Jesus surrender His own life on the cross as the ultimate sacrifice, they must have felt confused, devastated, and vulnerable. The chief priests even went to Pilate and asked him to place soldiers by the tomb in case the disciples tried to "steal the body and tell the people that he has been raised from the dead" (Matt. 27:64). But it was never going to be by force or deception that the followers of Jesus would experience restoration. It would be through the power of Christ to roll back the stone. It would be through our willingness to confess our sins and lay our own offering on the altar of our life.

Our passage today is not one we typically read on Holy Week, but this letter written to the early Christians reminds us that walking a life in the example of Jesus is hard. We will fall. We will make mistakes. We will fail to be obedient. But we are also gifted with a community of other believers who are there to encourage us and lead us to confession.

I can only imagine the conversation the disciples were having after Jesus was placed in the tomb and as they gathered together. Were they comforting each other? Reflecting on all that Jesus had taught them? Or did they feel vulnerable? When this happens to us, it's important that we have a small discipleship band or accountability group where we can confess our shortcomings, our sins, and our insecurities. Our sin will grow in the darkness, but salvation comes in the light that Jesus brings. As our brothers and sisters wander, we can bring light into their darkness through prayer and forgiveness. Our lives are the altars where we choose to lay our lives down for Christ as He laid His life down for us. Every time we share our hearts with other believers and confess our sins, we are practicing surrender and we are being transformed. As we wait for Christ to come again, let us band together with other believers to shine the light of the Holy Spirit on each other and for the world to come to know the Lord.

THE PRAYER

Lord, in the waiting may we find peace. In the silence of the dark tomb may we hold on to hope. As the dawn breaks may the light of Your victory be the light of our salvation. Amen.

THE QUESTIONS

- Is there any reason you would not feel comfortable confessing your sins to another person?

- If you are already in a discipleship band, what is the biggest benefit you have experienced? If you are not in a discipleship band for accountability, are you ready to join one? Check out discipleshipbands.com.

Day 47

Altar'd

MATTHEW 28:1-7 After the Sabbath, at dawn on the first day of the week, Mary Magdalene and the other Mary went to look at the tomb.

There was a violent earthquake, for an angel of the Lord came down from heaven and, going to the tomb, rolled back the stone and sat on it. His appearance was like lightning, and his clothes were white as snow. The guards were so afraid of him that they shook and became like dead men.

The angel said to the women, "Do not be afraid, for I know that you are looking for Jesus, who was crucified. He is not here; he has risen, just as he said. Come and see the place where he lay. Then go quickly and tell his disciples: 'He has risen from the dead and is going ahead of you into Galilee. There you will see him.' Now I have told you."

CONSIDER THIS

Something has changed. The women didn't even realize it when they got up that morning to go attend to Jesus's body.

They had been walking with Jesus, listening to His teachings, and being amazed at His miracles. Every day they had been with Jesus, learning from Him and living as His disciples. But today, something changed. What a difference a day makes. Only yesterday we were waiting, gathering with others and remembering Jesus's words. Yesterday we were hoping, but today we holler "Hallelujah!" The power of God has been proven. Christ the Lord has altered the course of history to fulfill His promise of salvation had been accomplished.

We began a Lenten journey just a few short weeks ago, longing to encounter God. On Ash Wednesday we set out to experience God as the Tailor of our lives. We committed to creating space in our lives and in our hearts as we made our lives an altar. We pledged to sacrifice ourselves, surrender the burdens we were carrying, and to confess our sins. And we anticipated a transformational shift that the Lord has promised as we desired to see earth as it is in heaven. Have we seen the transformation or have we been like the women who walked each day with Jesus not realizing that God was at work even when they didn't recognize it?

Let's return to the Tailor. Step once again onto the platform and look in the mirror. What do you see? Yes, of course, there is still work to be done, but do you not see it? Do you see the new creation of Christ? Do you see the grace that was poured out on you and is making all things new? Do you see the alterations that the Lord has been making as you have walked with Him faithfully each day? I do!

Today, we sing Hallelujah and remember that Christ is risen; He is not lying in a tomb as a piece of history, but He is the risen Savior who brings resurrection power to our lives today. We are no longer slaves to our sin, but we are forgiven and made new. The enemy cannot hold us down by our mistakes because we have been released from captivity by the crucified and resurrected King. It's Sunday and we are Easter people transformed by the love of Christ. Through His victory over death and the power of the Holy Spirit, we have been altar'd.

THE PRAYER

You are the risen Lord and we shout our praises to You! You are not in the tomb; You have risen from the grave! Teach us to live as Easter people every day and make our lives an altar to You! Amen.

THE QUESTIONS

- Acknowledge the changes, big and small, that the Lord has made in you through Lent. What changes are you most thankful for?
- How can you take the lessons you have learned about surrender and keep them in your daily practice?
- Who will you share your transformation story with this week?